MURALS
OF
THE MIND

MURALS

OF

THE MIND

Image of a Psychiatric Community

JAY HARRIS

and CLIFF JOSEPH

INTERNATIONAL UNIVERSITIES PRESS, INC.

New York

Murals of the mind: image of a psychiatric community.

Bibliography: p.
1. Schizophrenia. 2. Group psychotherapy.
I. Joseph, Cliff, joint author. II. Title.
[DNLM: 1. Psychotherapy, Group. 2. Schizophrenia—
Therapy. 3. Therapeutic community. WM203 H314m 1973]
RC514.H33   616.8'982'06   72-8793
ISBN 0-8236-3490-6

Manufactured in the United States of America

To people
who in their gathering of light
illuminate the creative process.

CONTENTS

If GROUPS could dream—and they can—and if the dream could be developed like a photographic print—and it can—then the onlookers could peer deep into the imaged self of the group—and we can. The group may be likened to an artist who, confounded by reality, reaches back inside in search of the means for shaping his wish to master reality. The shape he creates is the image he has of himself which we see realized in the group. The murals of his mind are two-dimensional frames, negatives perhaps, of a single stage in the moving sequence of his development. Each stage is a vital element in a naturally unfolding, self-creating process.

The mural of the group is a true expression of its existence, more lucid than an individual's manifest dream, more immediate. It portrays the structure of the group; it binds the feeling of the group; it preserves the imagery of the group. When people must live together in common circumstance a dynamic equilibrium ensues. A collective self emerges, which, fueled by the aggressive energy possessed by each member becomes a group institution.

Gradually, psychoanalysis has turned its attention to certain structures in the ego called self-representations and object representations. These have been considered theoretical structures because, as hypothetical constructs, their existence must be inferred. Such structures are analogous to subatomic particles whose existence is postulated in terms of their effect. Freud has described the shadow of the lost object being cast upon the ego, inferring that some new intrapsychic structure, derivative of the real object was affecting the ego. In *Group Psychology and the Analysis of the Ego* Freud (1921) stated, "A primary group of this kind is a number of individuals who have substituted one and the same object for their ego ideal and have consequently identified themselves with one another in their ego" (p. 116). If the word "self" is substituted for the word "ego" in this formulation, then the concept of a unified "group self" emerges. The authors believe that the group-mural technique, on which the current volume focuses, reveals the presence of self- and object representations within the context of the group's common representation of itself, just as a cloud chamber with appropriate electrical fields directs the previously inferred, but invisible particles against a photographic plate where their image is captured.

The authors would like the viewer to perceive the group as subculture. It becomes sharply delineated because our method of cultural analysis brings it into focus. This method attempts to discern three particular parameters of a subculture's momentary existence: the direction of the aggressive forces, the type of structural boundaries defining the subculture, and the representational nature of an immediate product of the whole subculture. A regular and periodic sampling of these parameters adds a temporal dimension to the continuously emerging identity of the group.

Psychoanalytic theory has come to view, as one of the impelling forces in schizophrenic disintegration, the loosing of relatively primitive aggression within the ego. This in turn induces a regressive primitivization of the existing ego structures. The clear light in which the mural presents group ego structures allows for an elucidation of the relationship between structure and aggression as periods of group regression occur. Thus the onlooker can actually view the process of structural disintegration in schizophrenia as it emerges in the period of the group's own structural regression.

THIS BOOK relates a group's structure to its imagery. The authors have employed a relatively modern technique referred to as "group mural." For 52 consecutive weeks the inpatients on the psychiatric ward of a university hospital, fictitiously named Theodore Herzl Hospital, produced such a mural as a cooperative exercise. Each mural session began with a group discussion, the purpose of which was to select a theme, continued with the actual production in pastel chalks on a large blank cardboard and ended with a discussion of the mural's merits and meaning. The entire process was recorded by a nonparticipating, note-taking staff member.

It was felt that in order to fully appreciate the meaning of the imagery as well as the group structure which evolved, there had to be a clear understanding of the reality scene out of which the group operated. The history of the ward was recreated for the year in question (August, 1966 to August, 1967) by studying the available written reports and by retrospective interviews with the staff. The context of the mural was further clarified by a detailed examination of the individual contributions of three patients. Their stays overlapped to include the entire year.

Our major finding is that in dealing with reality problems, such as a large influx of new patients or the absence of a head nurse, the group undergoes an identifiable and invariant sequence of responses. Each mural reveals a stage in the sequence of creative response to the ward problem. The stages follow:

1. Realism.
2. A statement of the problem in disguised form.
3. Defense against the problem.

4. Unconscious response to the problem.

5. A recombination of symbols to reapproach reality.

6. Resolution.

This sequence occurred consecutively, eight times, over the course of a year's murals. The nature of such sequences and their component stages are examined. It is concluded that these stages are the elements of the mechanism of identification. At an ego-psychological level, this mechanism is applicable to either individuals or groups.

When the particular sequences are identified and viewed as problem and resolution, a clear picture of group structural change emerges. Essentially, for the first six months, the group movement was one of growth and development. The growth was entirely analogous to the ego development of a young child. On the ward these months were characterized by the presence of a ward director and a head nurse who enforced the appropriate suppression of hostility. The latter six months reveal a process of group structural disintegration, almost specifically undoing the earlier development. This disintegration followed the de facto absence of the ward director and the illness of the chief nurse. The process of structural disintegration is considered as a case of group pathology equivalent to an episode of group schizophrenia.

1

THE DEVELOPMENT
OF GROUP CONSCIOUSNESS

Setting

IN LATE JULY, 1966, Dr. Isaacson sends letters to the faculty of medical colleges and to members of psychiatric associations in the New York Metropolitan area announcing the opening of psychiatric services at Theodore Herzl Hospital, a recently established university hospital. The new ward, 12-N, will be devoted to the long-range task of treating patients by psychoanalytically oriented psychotherapy within the framework of a therapeutic community. Close liaison with the referring physician and continuity of care using the resources of the outer community are stressed, but the brunt of the inpatient treatment will be borne by an on-going permanent staff. Prolonged stays for patients and staff will provide the necessary conditions for group formation in an institutional setting.

The new service brings further title to an already opulent psychiatric empire. A mile to the south, Charity Hospital, a huge city hospital, holds three floors of diverse psychiatric services. The nerve center of the entire Herzl psychiatric complex is clustered in several offices on the ground floor level.

The director of the complex, a psychoanalyst, has conscientiously synthesized teaching and research, training and service, community and individual orientation, into a department of national reputation. Further to the south, another large hospital, this one private, shares faculty and know-how. It is a fertile affiliation, bearing especially sophisticated neurophysiological research. A mile to the west of Herzl Hospital is a state psychiatric hospital, a pioneer not only in terms of its proximity to the people it serves, and in its organizational infrastructure, reflecting the macrostructure of the community, but in its absolutely filial relation to the Herzl complex, a relationship transcending the usual boundaries of state and city cooperation. A mile to the north is a psychiatric day center, steeped in group experience, extending into the surrounding community with apartments and a half-way house, recipient of the national government's earliest monetary recognition. It is Herzl's oldest child, already mature but in actual years not yet pubescent.

Further to the north, Lafayette Hospital, a city hospital affiliation department, is experimenting with a revolutionary method in the midst of a landmark slum area. Just as battlefield psychiatry has demonstrated the advantage of crisis intervention at the front lines, this department organizes and trains community members whose jobs are on the front lines—policemen, bartenders, teachers. Almost next door to Herzl Hospital is the Herzl Medical School, itself a branch of a large university. Its medical students are known for their interest in psychiatry, manifested both in their unusually high nationally tested aptitude scores and in the fact that fully a quarter to a third of its graduates are bound for the field. On faculty are meritorious researchers, especially productive in the field of ego-psychological aspects of child development. A separate hospital for the study and treatment of brain-damaged children awaits its moment of procreation.

The planning of the unit originated several years earlier when a floor was set aside for psychiatry during the designing of the hospital. As construction proceeded, a steering committee was set up, composed of several university psychiatrists experienced in inpatient services.

The special planning for 12-N's physical environment and its milieu begins in intermittent stages with the steering committee, and continues on a weekly basis, for a few months before the opening, with meetings of the administrative staff of the new unit. Those present at the administrative meetings are:

Dr. Isaacson	Director
Dr. Augress	Fellow
Miss Conrad	Head Nurse
Dr. Simon	Assistant Director
Dr. Evans	Admissions Director
Dr. Lukens	Fellow
Mr. Gordon	Social Worker
Miss Callahan	Occupational Therapist
Mr. Blackman	Art Therapist
Miss Marsh	Assistant Head Nurse

Staff

Dr. Isaacson, director of psychiatric services in the Herzl Hospital, has had a distinguished career, particularly marked by several directorships or assistant director positions throughout the country. His publications and interests center on liaison psychiatry, the emotional problems and therapy of persons with acute medical or surgical problems. He notes at the outset of his contact with the staff of 12-N that the longer a patient stays in an institution such as theirs, the better the prognosis for recovery. Dr. Isaacson is middle-aged, warm in personal contact and moderately distant in his leadership role. His attention is divided from the outset as he must deal with the establishment of an inpatient service at the same time that he is setting up a liaison service. Influential relatives of patients, benefactors and members of the Herzl Board, feel free to consult with him about every aspect of their relatives' care.

Dr. Schwartz, who becomes his assistant after several months, has been associated with the Herzl complex for about 10 years. He is tender, but tough, and very sensitive to the subjective experience of schizophrenic people. As he supervises the treating physicians, he emphasizes an empathic but objective concern. He is interested in the nature of creativity and in cognitive development, especially insofar as these processes are pathologically affected in schizophrenia. He conducts a weekly seminar in these problems for the edification of the staff and to further develop his own awareness.

Dr. Evans is interested in the therapeutic aspects of treating persons with an incipient schizophrenic illness. Functioning as the admitting psychiatrist, he selects patients of this sort whenever possible. He is imbued with a respect for sincere psychiatric facilities such as Chestnut Lodge or Austin Riggs and hopes to model Ward 12-N along the lines of such a treatment center. With his analytic mind and a maverick intellectual style, Dr. Evans appreciates the flow of popular culture transmitted by the young patients; he encourages them to express all the vitality that activates their defiance. His permissiveness often brings him into conflict with personnel whose orientation is more structured.

Dr. Lukens found Ward 12-N a propitious postresidency continuation of his psychiatric training. His interest in research is a self-styled way of objectifying his interest in the nature of mental life, and his theorizing is a way of transforming his experience to give it a further level of meaning. He would like to extend psychoanalytic thought further into the realm of the relatively static and enduring structural components of the ego. Self- and object images, as they are manifested in schizophrenic pathology, hold an innate fascination for him.

Dr. Augress, an associate of Dr. Isaacson, is a pragmatic, friendly South American. He is somewhat uneasy because all the other doctors have trained in the complex, while his background is more diverse. During the period of interpersonal staff subgroupings with the attendant inevitable gossip, he is friendly to all, while at the same time remaining aloof. For him, 12-N is a nexus of his career.

Miss Callahan, head of occupational and recreational therapy, trained and worked at the large city hospital affiliate of Herzl. Previously, her optimism and her enthusiasm for life were expressed in her work with adolescents. Her readiness to deal with adults on 12-N reflects an expanding maturity. Her marriage in 1969 to one of her co-workers is one of several romances which take root on 12-N.

Mr. Blackman is a successful black artist and an entrepreneur of the spirit. His revolutionary fervor takes him to an almost radical departure from society, but the outcome of his endeavors is always characterized by a real involvement with the problems of "the people." On the ward he is cool and methodical, sensitive, but very self-contained.

Miss Conrad, the head nurse, has worked with Dr. Augress and Dr. Isaacson in another setting. Although a recent graduate, she is self-assured, organized, stately, and more oriented to the real effect of behavior than to its unconscious motivations. Her rapport with Dr. Isaacson is never questioned.

Miss Marsh, her assistant, is more expressive. She deeply wishes to be a nurse who involves herself with her patients, helping them to grow toward a richer emotional experience. She has also worked at the city hospital of Herzl and she knows and respects much of the staff.

Having lived in the neighborhood of Herzl for many years, she feels especially at home in the new setting.

Mr. Gordon, the social worker, is a mature therapist. He is very diligent and capable of helping the staff to focus its work. Living in the suburban area where Dr. Schwartz and Dr. Isaacson also reside, he relates in a friendly social way with them outside of the ward setting. After two years he becomes involved in a research effort which addresses itself to the geographic movements of the patients on the ward in order to assess their social relationships from the point of view of a territorial imperative.

Mrs. Rohmer is a black aide who quietly draws together that portion of the staff which is awed by the relative affluence of the setting. Her maternal influence is exerted with the implicit approval of Miss Marsh. It is her son, who comes to a Christmas party on the ward in 1966, and who secretly marries Miss Serena, a focal patient for this story.

Miss Spodney is a dedicated nurse, a friend of Miss Conrad who comes to 12-N later in the year. She remains undecided as to whether her preferred role should be one of greater structure or closer emotional contact with the patients. Her own interest in painting leads to a special interest in the mural group and results in her cooperation with Mr. Blackman in treating patients by this modality.

The Patients/A Dramatis Personae

Miss Allen—An 18-year-old, acting-out college student who was much admired by the younger patient population. She in turn admired Mr. Phillips, the patients' paternal protector.

Miss Bernard—One of the triumvirate with Mrs. Cooper and Miss Serena. She made a serious suicide attempt just prior to taking her oral examination for a Ph.D. in sociology. She used sarcasm as a way of keeping most people at a safe distance.

Mr. Braverman—A middle-aged family man, who was dominated by his business partner and who longed to re-establish his authority after a business failure.

Mrs. Butler—A schizophrenic woman, who longed for closeness, but recurrently fled from her surroundings.

Mrs. Cooper—A depressed, young middle-class mother who had a need to prove that she was well-organized through organizing others. She vied constantly for the position of group leader. One aspect of her need to control was to prevent the expression of hostility. She was one of the triumvirate, along with Miss Bernard and Miss Serena.

Mr. Foley—A creative, unmanageable drug cultist; advocate of anarchy.

Miss Foster—A middle-aged social worker with a handicap, who treated her fellow patients as though they were handicapped. Despite a long stay on the ward, she experienced difficulty in acknowledging her status as a patient.

Mrs. Goodhart—A very rich, chronically treated woman, trying to achieve identity as a mother despite severe emotional deprivation in her childhood.

Mrs. Grier—First patient on the ward, elderly, depressed and mildly senile.

Mrs. Hecht—An intense, frustrated Hungarian editor, who underwent a dramatic decompensation which reflected the ongoing ward dynamics.

Miss Hirsh—An obese college student who went away to college to get away from her mother, only to find loneliness and unhappiness. She compensated for her physical problem with an intellectual grandiosity.

Miss Jacobs—A seriously ill acting-out adolescent, who enacted the dual roles of Mr. Foley's ward sister and girl friend, despite her feelings of inner despondency.

Miss Kurtz—A sarcastic older woman, who by her hostile remarks in the mural sessions, reveals her feelings of alienation from the younger members of the group.

Miss Meyers—A much institutionalized, but still provocative, young woman, whose boisterous profanities alternated with quiet entreaties for care.

Mr. Novick—An addicted and unsuccessful artist, whose mental suppleness launched him into a position of tyrannical proportions in the patient group, and whose slow downfall from this position constituted an essential element in the group's evolution.

Mr. Perlin—A whimsical, hypochondriacal student. Ambivalent protege of Mr. Novick.

Mr. Phillips—A depressed but intensely competitive business man, who practices his subtle manipulation of people during his stay on the ward. After he directed Mr. Novick's "demise," the patients uniformly looked to him for leadership.

Mrs. Polanski—A European stranger to this country (U.S.A.), who was victimized by the Nazi occupation as a child and who is now reacting to severe physical illness with aggressive tantrums. She had a tendency to introduce war themes into the murals.

Mrs. Popodopolus—A perceptive, ambivalent involutional woman, gratified by Mr. Novick's demise.

Mr. Rappaport—A relatively isolated and compulsive man, who at the retirement age became reactively more withdrawn.

Miss Richards—An adorable but acutely troubled adolescent, who wanted to create a family scene, with Mrs. Hecht as her mother, Dr. Schwartz as her father and the other patients as her siblings.

Mr. Ronan—An 18-year-old college student, extremely psychotic, with elaborate suicidal preoccupations, and given to macabre behavior such as emulating ghosts.

He was very active in the mural sessions, often drawing mirror images of his own face.

Miss Selig—A chronic schizophrenic adolescent who was
extremely regressed and whose interest was revived
only when she heard one of the famous "Beatles,"
whom she adored.

Miss Serena—A young, vivacious Afro-Latin, with borderline psychosis. An original Medicaid patient, and a
favorite of the nurses' aides, she is also one of the
triumvirate, together with Mrs. Cooper and Miss Bernard.

Miss Siegel—A petite but vey explosive schizophrenic
woman, whose dynamic behavior in the group was often influenced by her imaginary companions.

Mrs. Wilde—An eccentric Austrian woman, who would
have been a duchess had she remained in Austria; her
regal airs and imperious mannerisms had a bizarre
quality, which both bothered and amused her fellow
patients.

Mrs. Woodward—A wealthy alcoholic who had a need
to minimize the importance of the nurses, in order to
maximize her own sense of worth. She maintained an
air of mysterious suffering which, in her opinion,
justified her addiction to alcohol.

Society

A tone of social disruption permeates the consciousness of the people of the United States in the summer of
1966. The nation is increasingly divided into "hawks"
and "doves" over the war in Southeast Asia. After several
years of concerted exercise of United States military
power, its efficacy is being seriously questioned. The
President vacillates more as the limitation of military

power is increasingly argued. The summer of 1966 through the following summer is witness to the greatest numerical expansion of US war forces, although it is also the year in which the military can no longer be assured of full support. The Joint Chiefs wish to mobilize the reserves. As more people are directly affected, the disillusionment with power, with leadership and with the "American way of life" grows. The young people are dropping out with an air of condemned celebration. The new blacks, disenchanted with the "great society" as the economy diverts to war, plot retribution for the past. Psychiatry itself is divided as individual, group and community adherents vie for intellectual support and government grants.

The tone of doubtful power, "moral decline," and revolutionary consciousness cannot fail to permeate any group within the culture. The patients and staff who come to 12-N reflect the ferment and division in society. "Liberated flower children" and aged writers, addicts and housewives, doctors and students, Medicaid recipients and millionaires all convene under one roof.

The Ward's Fate

Before the wishes of "Mazel-tov" have died down, the good fortune of 12-N takes a slow but inevitable turn. Sudden illness strikes the director of the Herzl complex. No one knows whether he will be able to resume his chairmanship. As the months pass, the next echelon is strained and reluctant to make plans. There are tentative power realignments. As no clarification comes, each division of Herzl seeks its own autonomy. The State Hospital, still expanding, develops its own residency program aided by Herzl's good name. The Lafayette Hospital affiliate to the north, caught in the fervor of its own plans, finds that the spearhead of revolution can be directed inward as well as outward. Eventually, the community organizers attempt to wrest control, a movement that draws its strength from other events in society. Consequently, this department is virtually torn from the Herzl fabric. Efforts at repair founder as government aid is jeopardized.

In the midst of these disintegrating forces, the new ward finds itself increasingly isolated. Worse, Herzl Hospital and its university sponsors have overcommitted their resources. Financial confusion ensues and grows to crisis proportions. Accounting is entangled and corrupted. Government funds are diverted and misallocated. The new assistant dean, ambitious and aware, is inimical to long-term psychotherapy at the Herzl Hospital. He insists that 12-N would better serve the community if its emphasis were not long-term insight oriented, but better attuned to a general hospital's needs for organic modes of short-term treatment. No consistent or impelling voice is raised in the dean's council to avert 12-N's fate. After four years, as the assistant dean becomes dean, 12-N is forced to retire from psychiatric service. Space is allocated more economically to provide medical and surgical beds.

Theory

A conventional psychoanalytic orientation to understanding people works best in an atmosphere of stable social conventions. Especially when they are faced with the disrupting identity, the shifting moods and the dissembling music of the "flower children," Dr. Evans and Dr. Lukens find in their discussions that their theoretical understanding of schizophrenia is insufficient. The phenomena of these diverse patients, together with these diverse social elements, all come into focus in the weekly mural sessions. Hence it becomes necessary to fashion a theoretical approach to schizophrenia which can view the disease with equal relevance as a social or individual development.

Schizophrenia

This book approaches schizophrenia from the point of view of ego psychology. For the most part it is the mental *structures* (i.e., memory traces, images, representations, incorporated social elements) which we are considering, rather than the ego *functions* (i.e., reality testing, perception, motility, etc.) characterizing the patients on Ward 12-N. It is the change in the form and presentation of these structures in response to aggressive conflicts which is highlighted in the murals. The murals constitute an instrument for examining the schizophrenic fragmentation of individual patients as well as elements of social schizophrenia existing on the ward. They are well suited to this purpose because each individual contributes fragments to the mural which relate directly to structures in his own ego, as well as to the common theme.

The schizophrenic experience is considered here as a regressive response to drive states toward the self or toward another person which the ego finds unacceptable. In this view, the ego defensively reverts to earlier, more primitive forms of differentiation of its structures. The functions of the ego are also severely affected as a result of this regression. Reality testing and the capacity for object relations are compromised and the difficulty in these functions as well as the decrease in the ego's organizing and synthesizing ability feed back to undermine the use of the regressed structures which are now organizing the person's experience.

To illustrate further, the threat of loss of a person who has become essential to the operations of one's own ego, or the threat of encroachment by another person in such a way that the self feels an imminent loss of autonomy is an important source of an increasing and overwhelming sense of anxiety. This anxiety is experienced as a threat to the continuing existence of that part of the ego which has differentiated into the "self," and which is experienced by the person as the executor of intentions and other drive derivatives. This form of anxiety, originating in the infant's repeated experience of self-extinction and the attendant helplessness, is conceivably just as basic as castration anxiety, separation anxiety, fear of the superego, or fear of loss of love. It is specific to the fear of loss of autonomous mental functioning, such functioning being dependent on the integrity of the basic structures. At the instigation of this threat, a regressive defense is mobilized such that the self reverts to more archaic functional structures.

Attendant upon the reduced ability to direct discharge processes, the ego's ability to bind stimulation and to synthesize percepts from the data of sensation is diminished. Stimuli are experienced as painful and uncontrollable and the basic data of mental contents lose their relevance. The cognitive mode becomes less abstract and increasingly pervaded by drive derivatives. As self-structure within the ego loses its differentiation, the ability to delineate external from internal stimuli contracts, a defect in reality testing. The area of regression considered most pertinent to understanding schizophrenia and certainly most pertinent to this book concerns the dedifferentiation of self and object structures.

The self, although it is partially derived through identifications with the external object, can function to organize inner experience because of its subjective equivalence to consciousness. The present thesis holds that the utility of the self is inherent in its function of organizing consciousness. Drive derivatives are sensed by consciousness and their qualities are organized by the self. In

Chapter Seven of *The Interpretation of Dreams,* Freud (1900) considers consciousness as deriving from the functioning of an organ of perception which is directed to the inside of the mental apparatus. Just as percepts derived from other senses are organized into potentially meaningful percepts, the self organizes the data of internal energy into a form meaningful to the perceiving consciousness. The energy available to direct conscious-perception may be called a hypercathexis. In his book on dreams, Freud depicts a barrier, a kind of censor operating between a system consciousness and the verbal system of the pre-conscious. He postulates that attention (hypercathexis) is necessary to transcend this final barrier to the access for discharge. Attention is also a function of the experiencing self which discriminates among the various possibilities of action (alternative drive discharge). In this book, self is taken as the immediate superordinate organizing aspect of the ego; that is, a subjective consciousness which judges the pleasure or pain inherent in an intention. Part of the experience of self is related to the ability to conceive of an intention. It is precisely this ability which is lost in schizophrenia. Consequently, the schizophrenic person is rendered essentially passive.

In incipient schizophrenia, the ego attempts to preserve its essential self-structure. Imagery relating to the self is experienced more acutely and identifications are enhanced in order to reinforce the structure of the self; but, like the accretion of calcium on a bone in Paget's disease, it becomes a dysfunctional organ, a looming appendage of the mind. The nature of the self-experience is increasingly one of conscious pain as the possibility of discharge is felt to be blocked. The withdrawal of object cathexis into narcissistic ego cathexis, although relevant, approaches the subject from an angle different from that which is presently applied. Intense narcissism often lapses into equally intense experiences of shame and humiliation as the self loses its sense of subjective utility. Drive derivatives are still pressing for discharge but they can no longer be structured into patterns suitable to represent acts or intentions. The ability to discriminate between possible actions and their relationship to reality is progressively lost. The hierarchy of possible acts ordinarily organized by the self becomes an indiscriminate assemblage. Either all acts are blocked or they break through with primitive force (defused energy). The loss of discharge capability in the self-structure promotes a split between the essentially expressive and the essentially sensation-organizing side of the self. This split has been referred to as a split in the ego, or a split between feeling and intellect, but within the context of this book it refers to a split in the self-structure, between the objective or sensory-derived aspect, and the subjective or expressive discharge aspect. This division undoes the work of identification.

Self- and object representations refer to highly organized attitudes which can be objectively verified. The representations are rooted in self- and object images, which in turn are derived from memory images and sensations. The representations serve to structure the incoming data of perception while they bind drive energy, providing a kind of pyramidal channeling which serves to organize impulses toward meaning and potential consciousness.

As Hartmann (1950) points out, the self is the repository in the ego of large amounts of instinctual energies, which are neutralized to a greater or lesser degree, thereby becoming available to the ego for its various functions. The self-structure develops in integrated stages, each synthesis resulting in further supplies of energy which can be utilized by the ego. Even when synthesized at its most mature level, the self continues to be recreated as the person undergoes aggressive and sexual conflicts which find their resolution in discharge possibilities patterned by the renewed or changing self-structure. Instinctual energies are viewed as broadly bound in the following series of integrations:

1. Synthesis of a maternal image out of the impinging diversity of stimuli.
2. Synthesis of a body image.
3. Synthesis of separate self- and object images.
4. Synthesis of abstract representations of these structures.

Each synthesis is modelled on a new identification which provides a relatively enduring structure for the organization of drive energies. As is true of an artistic creation, each successful synthesis yields pleasure because energy can be liberated by the new economy of means. For instance (see number four above) the synthesis of diverse self-images into a more unified self-representation is subjectively experienced as an increment in consciousness. Similarly, the creation of a self which is autonomous and separate from the image of mother (see number three above) yields greater discharge possibilities because the object need no longer be present in order for gratification to occur. In this connection a psychoanalytic hypothesis holds that there is a time in infancy when self and mother are not yet viewed as separate mental entities. At such a stage the feeling of satisfaction of drive states is oriented toward the mother who is experienced as an extension of need. In number 2 above, disparate vestibular, kinesthetic and affective feelings are experienced in terms of separate body parts and zones at first. Then as the body of the self is *identified* with the externally perceived body of the object a synthesis of the body image can occur. This focuses potential actions in the direction of relevant discharge possibilities. The physical exertion necessary to attain gratification is lessened and the image of a complete body is the beneficiary of the new economy. Finally, in number one above, the synthesis of a maternal image allowing for her recognition is an early mental integration which permits of much conservation in the expenditure of perceptual energies, lessens frustration and yields available energy with which to infuse her mental image.

In schizophrenia, as self-representations are abandoned, the mature self-structure is no longer capable of structuring, absorbing and channeling the drive energies. As a result, they disrupt the ego's functional capacity until new psychic equilibrium is achieved whereby they can be contained and structured by some less differentiated self- or object structure. Those aggressive energies used in segregating and reinforcing mature mental representations are also released into the apparatus. Schizophrenic people, perceiving a radical change in their identity, commonly relate much of their experience to a feeling that their self is absent.

In order to compensate for these feelings of unreality and forestall the loss in ego control, they attempt to shift the focus of their experience to another person. The effect on their real relationship to external objects is an increased dependency, and concomitantly, the effect on their intrapsychic relationships is a tendency to fuse the image of self with that of an important object image. A typical complaint is that of being engulfed. This shift in the focus of their identity amounts to the initial stage of regression in the intrapsychic structured field. Harbingers of this stage are the detached heightening of self-consciousness, depersonalization and derealization. After the initial regression, further stages of ontological structural regression occur, manifested, for example, by pathological symptoms of disturbed body-image integration. All of the pathological symptoms of schizophrenia can be related in a direct way to the structural dislocations in in the person's inner world.

A reference to the case of Mr. Ronan, who is an 18-year-old admitted in the latter half of the year, can illustrate some of the above points. Mr. Ronan emphatically maintains that his self no longer exists. His solution to the problem of how to relate to the real world is to create what Laing (1960) describes as a false self-system. He constantly experiences in terms of other people. His urge toward identification can be viewed as an attempt to repair the self-structure, to recreate it anew in a more perfect form. In his treatment Mr. Ronan would repeatedly enact the identity of each member of his family. Similarly, he emulates the character of his therapist, Dr. Lukens. Mr. Ronan also sought the group of patients on 12-N as an inviting but fragmented set of images with which to identify. His attempt to invigorate his self-structure through a process of repeated primary identification with his objects is characteristic of schizophrenic people. Conceivably, this is a pathological exaggeration of the normal mechanism of intrapsychic structure formation.

Analysis of the murals and of the group interaction during the construction of the murals reveals a reciprocity of identifications. For instance, Mr. Ronan, despite his regressed state of ego functioning, served as an image of the group's character at times. Even when his body image as revealed in his mural contributions is fragmentary, the group can use it as a basis for their interrelating. Groups must have an innate capacity to function at various integrated levels.

Group

In *Group Psychology and the Analysis of the Ego,* Freud

(1921) makes the point that a group may be likened to an individual who exists in an unconscious relatively undifferentiated state. As with the individuation of a person, the unstructured group must first undergo a process of differentiation if it is to develop those attributes which will provide it with a structured, individualized identity. He asserts that the process for accomplishing this depends on the formation of libidinal ties between the members which are strong enough to overcome feelings of mutual antipathies. The feelings of hostility are overcome as the group members acquire common bonds of identification with a leader figure. These feelings can be repressed by placing the leader figure in a position equivalent to a person's ego ideal. The individual members feel an equivalence with each other, each in his own ego.

Freud wrote this paper prior to his definite allocation of the ego to the position of a structured entity. He did not distinguish formally between self and ego at this time. Given these distinctions, it is not unlikely that he would view the group as a structure which has acquired a common sense of self, dependent on a common relationship to the leader figure, who constitutes an object. The implications for the present exposition are manifold. First, if Freud is correct, the group in its structural evolution can be treated as if it were an individual. That is, the intrapsychic elements of ego structure, self- and object images, find a structural equivalent in the composition of the group's structure. Further, the process of identification can be considered a mechanism of structure formation with equal applicability to groups and to the individual. Finally, pathological changes affecting individual structural components of self and object should find their parallel application in group pathology.

As evidence for equating the "group mind" with an infantile person's mind, Freud cites a group member's

readiness to react in a primary-process fashion, impul-
sively and without rational logic. Further, the group is
overly suggestible, seeking comfort and omnipotent control. He states that in this condition the group seeks a
leader, either a real person, a potential person, or an ethi-
cal principle. The essence of the group's relation to its
leader is to be found in the identification mechanism, the
precursor in his view of all object relations. He states that
the outcome of identification can be pathological, as it is
in the state of melancholia when the identification is with
an object that is felt to be rejecting or absent. In Freud's
view the mechanism of identification is not thoroughly
worked out. He notes a readiness in individuals to fuse
recurrently with their own ego ideal; in the case of mania
this results in an euphoric energy release; in the case of
ego development it results in the object which has been
put in place of the ego ideal, leaving its mark on the person's own ego.

Freud believes that group members, in their common
identification with an ego ideal, derive a feeling of shared
substance. This is similar to his theory of the primal
horde cannibalizing the flesh of the father figure as each
acquires his characteristics. The evolution of a group is
mediated by its relationship to a leader figure just as a
child's ego development is mediated by the important
adult figures in his life.

The group on 12-N forms its structure in a series of
integrated steps which depend on its relationship to Dr.
Isaacson and to other leader figures. The staff and the
patient group evolve virtually equivalent structures.

As the group creates common images, the images are
incorporated into the self- and object structures of the
individual members. Personal identity formation, like the
structure of an organ in the body, is never complete.
Images are added and subtracted, constantly reintegrated

by the synthesizing ability of the person's ego organization. Group participation means, on the level of ego psychology, that common elements of identity are promoted. The acquisition of identity elements and the sense of a communal self in the group corresponds to experiences of individual development in a person's life history.

Experience with the group on 12-N and analysis of its artistic productions show that at a particular time the group functions at a particular level of maturity in regard to the level of meaning provided by its mutual object images. As the group evolves, stages in development are recapitulated which result in those kinds of integrations leading to the freeing of psychic energy. There is repeated recreation of the group's image of itself, each new synthesis binding the drive energies which were individually involved in some conflict which the group was undergoing.

The group, as it repeatedly turns its attention to threatening factors in its environment and to its own hostility, appears to collectively harness its energies, using its aggression first to turn away from the source of the problem and later to resynthesize a solution. This creative process is analogous to the hypothesized neutralization of energy in an individual. The group emerges from its confrontations with a common problem in reality with a change in its internal structure. Its individual members adopt common solutions consisting of the acceptance of new images of themselves and of the group, which serve to bind the energy of aggression that arose in them individually in response to the common problem. The emergence of a set of common symbols in the group allows for a more highly conscious form of communication. This is a process which can be considered as neutralization of aggressive energy by structure formation in the group.

In the latter half of the year in question, the group's

"self," or common set of imagery, loses its mature quality and a succession of regressive phases occurs. The group functions in its communication and in its artistic enterprise in a less highly integrated fashion. It undergoes a process of regression such that forms of integration which were built up are consecutively undone. Documentation of this process will be presented in the main body of this book. The libidinal element in the development of both patient and staff groups was less apparent and less well documented than the aggressive element. However, during the first six months a tone of some affection and mutual respect served to provide a constant background to the perpetuation of the process of identification and to the overcoming of hostile feelings. In the troubled later months, there is a longing to return to the earlier conditions.

An ego psychological approach to schizophrenia, to individual development and to group formation has been indicated here. Such an approach has the advantage of allowing an analogous examination of individuals and groups in terms of their structure formation. This approach has been necessitated by the nature of the material which emerges in examining the individual patients, their group interaction and their collective mural production within the total milieu of Ward 12-N.

Essentially, the concept of self can be applied in relation to a group as well as an individual because the intrapsychic self includes an element which is externally derived, which provides structural organization and which can be borrowed from other group members, especially the leader. The internally derived drive or affective element of the self is bound to this organization in parallel ways through similar experiences of stimulation in group members. This interface of self, where intentions are structured as the drive derivative emerges, is the surface of conscious experience. The existence of a common consciousness is easily inferred by group members. When empathic communication occurs among members of the group, group structure is created. When communication occurs intrapsychically, at the self's interface, an identification is created.

2

THE WARD'S HISTORY

THERE IS a considerable invitation to regressive expression in a mural group. Group participation in itself is conducive to regressive phenomena. The purpose of the group preempts the integrating function of the self, evoking infantile expectations of parental influence. Expression in the visual mode is also closer to earlier modes of mental function. As Bertram Lewin (1969) notes, people gradually progress in their internal mode of mental representations from overt visual hallucination, to visual imagery when a self is differentiated, to a more abstract mode of internal representation. The task of depicting group themes in visual images would be expected to reveal a great deal about the undercurrents of group life. Mural, or wall drawing, also reduces the dimensions of perceptual reality to a more primitive form.

Roots of Group Art

The idea of a group of people relating to each other for some creative purpose is ancient. For primitive peoples, group activity was a necessary way of life. It was important as early as prehistoric times for man to engage in socially oriented activities if only as a means of protection from the threatening elements and predatory beasts of his time. Although the basic communal need for survival was predominant, the secondary emotional rewards of social interaction must be seen as significant incentive for keeping the group going. Some form of enjoyment must have been shared by Cro-Magnon men as they hunted together in group security. Likewise the women, as they went about their collective agricultural and domestic chores. And children, of course, have always played together. But what about the artists of those early days?

We know that cave (mural) painting was one of the favorite creative activities of primitive man. Was this done individually or in groups? Assuming that man's artistic nature has not changed very much over the past one million odd years, we might expect that he had his times to work both individually and in group, depending on his need. Windels (1949) observes that cave painting such as that at Lascaux could only have been conducted through the collective will of the whole society. The technical problems alone would require the participation of many people helping the artist or artists. This speculation raises an interesting question regarding the origin of the group mural and leads us inevitably to wonder about the beginnings of group art therapy itself.

Obviously the terms mural, group, art and therapy were not part of Cro-Magnon's vocabulary. The concept of groups for the purpose of social intercourse was perhaps less important to him than to the more community-oriented man of the Neolithic Age to whom these words were equally unknown. Nonetheless it can be inferred that the basic need for mental as well as physical health was common to both early forms of man, and even without knowledge of the words, what we refer to here as "art" was important to his development. The wall drawings or murals which he has left behind bear witness to our supposition. At some point during the execution of his murals, he undoubtedly got together with other artists, for practical and technical assistance as well as for the reassuring sense that common enterprise can diminish the threat to survival. It follows then that these needs being met, what we refer to as the therapeutic experience must have resulted. Lewin (1969) in discussing the Lascaux murals concludes that the images probably served as a kind of communal "memory bank." In this case the murals would provide a channel of communication within the society, depicting a kind of group mind. Spanning aeons of time, from prehistoric to modern twentieth-century man, the paper mural devised for therapeutic and evaluative use in present-day clinical group situations may have a function not too different from that of the wall mural of prehistoric times.

Art, in addition to having its decorative, social and utilitarian functions, is extremely important as an expression of unconscious processes. Produced singularly by the individual, a work of art may serve as a conveyor of very deep personal concerns. Done in concert with a group of people, art may serve as an effective means of interpersonal communication for those who have trouble expressing their feelings in direct verbal encounter.

Periods of awkward silence often prevail when a group of people are brought together to share sympathetically in the airing of difficult problems. The introduction of a task into such a setting can provide the catalyst needed to evoke some meaningful exchange. In the furtherance of a creative end, an art-oriented task would seem to be a natural choice. It is difficult to pinpoint exactly when and by whom the choice was made to involve a group of people in the cooperative creation of a mural. Historical reference is given to group cooperation in the preparation and painting of Egyptian murals in the Middle Kingdom and the Empire. Master painters throughout art history frequently employed teams of apprentices to transfer their original cartoons to the surfaces of great walls too immense for the energies of a single individual, or too

THE WARD'S HISTORY 43

time consuming as in the case of popular renaissance painters besieged by numerous commissions. Groups of people have traditionally gathered together out of a common need and desire to give artistic expression to their feelings about life, themselves and each other. The group games of children and partying adults often take on this perfectly natural form. Even present-day advertising, with its "brain-storming" artistic cooperation, reflects the natural function of group art.

Margaret Naumberg (1966) and Edith Kramer (1958) in their divergent ways have led pioneer movements in the field of art therapy. Naumberg is known for her analytically oriented approach to art therapy, while Kramer is noted for her emphasis upon the importance of art. In her pioneering work at the Wiltwyck School for Boys, Kramer encouraged emotionally disturbed youngsters to gain self-awareness and stability through creative group involvement. Hanna Yaxa Kwiatkowska of the National Institute of Mental Health explored the use of art as a means of communication and self-expression within the family group. George R. Bach (1954) used a "round-robin" technique of group art therapy. Lynn Berger at the Einstein College of Medicine, Vera Zilzer at the Lincoln Community Mental Health Center and Elinor Ulman, Editor of the *American Journal of Art Therapy* and art therapist at D.C. General Hospital, all personally known by the author, are among the contributors of the numerous variations and group techniques developed by leading art therapists over the past 30 years.

Mechanical Structure for the Mural

Mr. Blackman comes to Ward 12-N prepared to set up group mural as a weekly activity, a project in which he has the cooperation of Miss Callahan, who heads up "O.T." (Occupational Therapy). He considers that six to

eight people is the ideal number of participants for a
group mural session. During the first two months in
which this technique is used on the ward, this is the
usual number of participants. However, as the ward's patient population increases, the number of participants
sometimes reaches 12 or 14.

Physically, the group mural setting may be structured
in a variety of ways. The media used to execute the
mural may range from wet to dry to plastic or a mixture
of these. At Herzl Hospital, the physical arrangement and
choice of materials were determined by the therapist after
careful consideration of such factors as the purpose for
which the activity was to be used, the amount of time to
be alloted for the session, floor space open for seating
and available wall space for mounting the mural panel.

In seeking to set the stage for the maximum degree of
group interaction, the semicircular seating arrangement is
by far the most effective since it allows each of the participants a full view of the mural panel and an opportunity
for greater visual contact with every other group member.
This arrangement is also useful in that it increases the
variability of nonverbal communication and heightens the
possibility of direct verbal exchange among group members. Semicircular seating also affords the therapist and
the recorder a better overall view of the facial expressions
and frontal gestures which serve as indicators of the patients' feelings and attitudes.

As there was no flat wall space of adequate size and
suitable location in the activity therapy room at Herzl
Hospital, it was necessary to mount the mural panel on a
portable 3' by 5' blackboard. This served as an excellent
carrier for the gray cardboard panel which was cut to the
same size and secured to the carrier with masking tape.
One advantage of using the portable blackboard is its
easy mobility for movement to other areas for the purpose of demonstration. The gray cardboard (the quality

of shirtboard) was selected by the therapist for its color neutrality, crudeness of texture (for use with pastels), durability and ease of storage when a proper receptacle is provided. The storage unit used at Hertzl made it possible to stand the panels on end horizontally. By attaching filing tabs at the top of each panel indicating its date and title, an orderly and efficient filing system was maintained.

Pastel was chosen for its depth of tone and brilliance of color. It was preferred for its relative simplicity, since it requires no mixing with water or solvents, needs no extra tools for its manipulation (e.g., brushes) and is less messy because it is a dry medium. Pastel also proved more useful in allowing the therapist to detect with greater accuracy such telling linear characteristics as might be smeared over with a brush or washed away in a cascade of running paint. The reference here is to the increased possibility of accident with wet media, rather than any deliberate alterations the patient might choose to make. Pastel was found to be the most reliable, for example, in the retention of significant details which expose the varying degrees of tension to be seen in the amount of pressure with which the medium is applied. The quality of weak, broken, shaky lines is more easily retained for comparison with stronger, more aggressive features. Upon completion of a mural, a liberal spray coat of fixative is always applied to insure against the distortion of significant details by accidental smudging.

There are three phases in each group mural session:

Phase I: Theme Selection

The theme or subject of the mural is selected by vote from among several suggestions contributed by group members. The therapist who is present attempts to maintain a completely neutral orientation to the themes and only enters into the discussion to try to keep the group goal oriented. Experience with group mural sessions shows that rejected themes are often related to accepted ones and make their way into the mural. Some themes recur from week to week, and even over longer time spans, as if awaiting their moment of expression. This is one of the factors instrumental in the emergence of the reconstruction of the ward's history. The murals are named, for identification purposes, by the group's chosen theme.

Phase II: Mural Production

In this phase, each member, according to his ability and inclination to participate graphically, contributes to the representation of the chosen theme. Sometimes the members choose to arrange their contributions in accordance with their seating arrangement. At times, two or more members contribute simultaneously. Sometimes one member will have a predominant effect. Again, the art therapist makes no attempt to intervene in these proceedings, except to maintain the goal orientation.

Phase III: Postmural Discussion

The group members discuss and interpret, if they choose, the meaning of their individual contributions as well as the significance of the total group production.

The observers of the group mural session include the art therapist, who facilitates the session, and a recorder. Each needs to be aware of such meaningful factors as attendance, seating patterns, whether the group achieves unity or is more inclined toward subgroupings in terms of age, sex, race, religion, familiarity with the setting, etc. They must ascertain whether the group becomes patient-centered (self- or peer-oriented) or therapist-centered (object- or authority-oriented) and whether there is a high or low level of interaction. It is important to observe who plays such roles as leader, scapegoat, monopolist, isolate, etc., as well as the quality and quantity of each group member's graphic contribution to the mural. With regard to the graphic contributions, such particulars as choice of color, area selected, object drawn and manner of execution are carefully noted.

The record of each mural session includes the mural itself as well as the recorded protocol. This protocol in the form of process notes constitutes the most important source of material for this book. Each patient's contribution is noted in the context of his relationship to the group.

Methods

At the time that the murals were executed, there was no expectation that they would form the basis for a critical study. The data was collected entirely as process notes for the therapeutic task of helping the patients to express themselves by this modality. Therefore, a retrospective study has been undertaken. This has the advantage of protecting the data from contamination by preconceived hypotheses. In this sense, it was a natural experiment. One disadvantage is that the history of events which occurred on the ward between July 1966 and July 1967 had to be reconstructed two years after they had taken place. Thus there may have been a certain amount of retrospective deletion and distortion.

The aim of the reconstruction is to understand the reality situation which confronted the ongoing participating group. Most of the original staff is still present two years later at the time when the reconstruction is organized. In addition to the mural records all of which are dated, indicating the participants and the surrounding circumstances, patients' charts are available for the cross-checking of events. There is also a partial record of memos pertaining to directives affecting the ward. The flow of patient admissions and discharges and the corresponding census are documented. Beyond the factual data, interviews are used to chronicle the ward's infancy.

Two group discussions are held with most of those who participated in the original administrative meetings. The first one is fairly expansive and there are even jokes made about the division of ideas and the philosophy of that time. Dr. Evans, with a fine eye for the ridiculous, leads the group in voicing feelings about the struggles of a new psychiatric unit and the sometimes unrealistic expectations. By contrast, the second meeting is humorless. The group questions the validity of this study. The time under discussion in this second meeting is the second six months of the ward's existence. Demonstrably, it is a period of regressive grievance among staff members of all disciplines which is exacerbated by shifting leadership. As the staff was unable to express its own angry bewilderment at that time, it still balks at such expression two years later.

The material gained from individual interviews is less guarded. Interviews are conducted with the Admissions Director, the Social Worker, the Chief of Occupational Therapy, the Art Therapist, the Ward Secretary, the Head Nurse, the Director, his former assistant and the Assistant Head Nurse. Each presents a wide range of evidence to demonstrate the problems of the unit's beginnings. After April of 1967 a communications log was developed. It documents reliably the events in the last three months of the study.

Validity

An essential accord emerges between data gathered in the reconstruction and mural data. The ward goes through repeated sequences of problem solving. As a problem emerges in reality, both the patient group and the staff group find it necessary to deal with the problem.

Eight sequences are identified through the year and in each one the mural documents a stage-by-stage response to the reality problem until a solution emerges. It is this documentation which constitutes the essence of the present volume and it is the invariant approach to the solutions documented by the murals which constitutes the internal validity for this study. Seen week-by-week in the context of their ongoing reality, the murals tell a unique story. It is the quality of being consistently overdetermined which gives the story its credulity. The authors are so impressed by the fixity of this phenomenon that they often cast their interpretations of individual murals in definitive terms.

Sequence

Each period in the ward's life comes to be defined by a moving sequence of approaches to the problems which exist. When the 50 murals are laid out for a comprehensive view of their totality, repeating patterns emerge. They arrange themselves into six different types which recur periodically. The first group is for the most part realistic; the second is characterized by barely disguised versions of reality (e.g. murals populated by animals). The next type of murals repeatedly expresses flight and fear; the fourth type presents an almost classical division between land and water, outside and inside, reality and feeling. Finally, types five and six portray recombination, restitution and resolution, a moving back toward the scene of reality.

What emerges in the panoramic view of the murals is an invariant sequence, a march of meaning precisely in the order that is enumerated above. The murals become a stark testimony to the operation of an invariant approach to the problems found in reality. When seen in this way, it becomes possible to correlate the reality events with the murals, because each sequence begins with a mural portraying a problem in reality and ends with a mural portraying the resolution of that problem. When this fact is clearly seen, then the problem and the resolution as defined by the murals can be compared with the findings of the reconstruction of the ward's first year. Knowing the place of the mural in the sequence provides an interpretive context.

History. In Chart 1 the year has been divided into eight naturally occurring periods with a summary of the events which are most pertinent to the staff's functioning during each period. At the same time, the chart summarizes the resolution which the patients depicted for the like period in the murals. This chart portrays several other concerns which will be worked out in detail. First, there is a meaningful accord in each period between the staff's problem and the patients' problem and resolution. The patients must approach their problems in a very concrete way and their feelings and the types of resolutions are most easily viewed from the point of view of infantile conflicts and complexes. The staff views itself at all times as a more rational entity, portraying its problems in the form of logical dilemmas. It will be seen, however, that staff and patients alike represent two levels of approach to the same reality, and the dynamic understanding which is worked out for one serves for both.

Period I. At the outset, both the patients and the staff are faced with the problem of forming a group out of unrelated individuals who as yet find one another's responses a mystery. More specifically, in forming a group the members must deal with the hope for satisfaction and the hostility which emerges. The staff divides itself into a more liberal and a more conservative "camp," differing especially in their respective approaches to hostility. Long hours are spent in administrative meetings in an attempt to determine how safe to make the ward and how to deal with suicidal or homicidal patients. There is also the ongoing but unannounced question of who will dominate: Group A which opts for the suppression of all hostility or Group B which seeks free verbal expression.

It is the patients who must live with the staff's decisions. For 24 hours a day they are faced with one another's unpredictable hostility. They must also form an entity which has an internal viability. As Chart 1 indicates, the patients resolve the problems of their first seven weeks on the ward by forming a diffuse, equal group with one division, based on whether they express or suppress a sense of individual frustration. This resolution will have more meaning to the reader as each mural session is described in greater detail.

It is a common observation by those concerned with ward management that the emotional tone of the patients reflects that which is present in the staff. This is a consistent finding for each period of the year in question, raising the issue of whether some generalized identification process is prevailing. The reasons for the parallels between staff and patient groups are multidetermined at many levels, and some of the reasons will be mentioned in relation to the initial period.

The staff and the patients, like any group of people living or working together, develop aggressive conflicts which require some control to prevent destructive outbreaks, and to channel the aggression in active pathways of mastery. The leader is automatically cast in the position of authority where he is expected to exert limitations on the flow of aggression. In such a role resentment and idealization inevitably accrue to him.

The style of leadership of the director, Dr. Isaacson, appears to be characterized by the firm suppression of hostility. Most of the staff members who were selected to work on the service seemed, in the opinion of the authors, to share an innate sense of reluctance to express hostile feelings. In this way there is a readiness to form a community which channels aggressive forces in common pathways. The staff communicates an atmosphere of firm control of hostility both by example and by confirming cooperative patient behavior. It builds a nucleus of such patients by "selecting" them for longer stays. The selection process exercised by the staff and Dr. Isaacson, and later by the patients themselves, is not entirely conscious. At the more concrete level of interpersonal relationships, particular patients and particular staff members discover mutual compatibilities. This tends to produce two groups which mirror one another. In later periods it becomes apparent that one patient is given the role of displaced staff leader; consequently patients and staff alike relate to him as such a figure.

The structural configurations in the patient and staff groups are also overdetermined. In that each therapist comes to be noted for the treatment of a particular type of individual, his patients come to represent that therapist in the interplay of the ward's life. One of the earliest patients, Miss Serena, whose socioeconomic background is lower class, becomes the favorite of the aides; her relationship to the other patients reflects the relationship of the aides to the other staff members. Particular nurses develop a wish to work with particular patients, usually on the basis of an identification mechanism. Thus, one nurse becomes involved in long intense discussions with a suicidal patient in the hope of "saving" that patient. She attempts to offer her own way of dealing with hostility to the patient. But the nursing staff itself is divided into two groups, one of which insists on the professional role-oriented approach to patient care as exemplified by Miss Conrad of Group A, while the other devotes itself to meaningful patient contact, as exemplified by Miss Marsh of Group B. The degree of personal contact with

patients becomes a matter of rational conjecture and discussion in ward meetings as to whether this is a positive
approach for the patient. Only to the extent that the
staff deals with its own division can this problem be
resolved. Other patients more frightened of any individual
contact are attracted to the control exercised by medication and by the efficient methods and structure which
Miss Conrad stands for. In this way, the patient group
evolves along a line of cleavage which reflects that of
the staff.

The year chosen is a convenient time to consider the
group's transformation because it begins at the actual
inception of the ward's life and it ends with the mass
exodus for vacations which prepares the ward for a new
beginning in the succeeding year. The first six months
differ basically from the second six months in that a
structure building process occurs at first, whereas that
structure is progressively destroyed in the latter months.
Each period is described in terms of the major staff
events which occur because such events circumscribe
the reality with which the patient group is dealing in the
murals.

Period II. As Chart 1 illustrates, the second period, occurring between September 22 and November 3, is one of
staff differentiation. After having evolved into a consciously defined entity composed of two subgroups, it
becomes necessary for the staff members to work out
their particular roles in relation to one another. A great
deal of energy is invested in learning the boundaries of
professional roles. For instance, if the patient does not
attend the beginning of a therapeutic activity, is it the
role of O.T. or that of the nurse to confront him? If a
nurse is working closely with a patient, should the nurse
be present when the patient is at a group activity? Who
should decide whether a patient can go on a planned

CORRELATION OF STAFF REALITY AND MURAL DEPICTION
THE WARD'S HISTORY

CHART I

Period	Staff Events	Patients' Resolution of Problems as Depicted in and Derived From the Mural
I:8–4–66 to 9–22–66	Staff split into "A" & "B" types re aggression.	Form a diffuse equal group with one division.
II:9–22–66 to 11–3–66	Staff role differentiation is catalyzed by erratic patients.	The oldest subgroup shows the way to individuated cooperation.
III:11–3–66 to 12–15–66	Isaacson's memos of authority. The centrality of two "older" nurses.	Protect each other, even from inner hurt.
IV:12–15–66 to 2–2–67	Isaacson withdraws; Schwartz adds authority. Staff preoccupation with Novick and Augress.	Elevate and scapegoat a new leader.
V:2–2–67 to 3–30–67	Nursing rebellion. Conrad's illness. Staff reaction to Hecht's symptoms.	Everyone becomes the leader through "killing" and "ingestion."
VI:3–30–67 to 4–27–67	Staff's helpless fascination with Foley. Marsh's decline.	The group abandons itself to the ravages of its own guilt.
VII:4–27–67 to 6–28–67	Salvatore's "madonna" era.	Rebirth by letting one member portray a mother. Hating her image after she leaves.
VIII:6–28–67 to 8–2–67	Staff dissolution through massive vacations.	Projecting archaic and powerful "good mother" images into the institution.

movie trip—therapist, O.T., a charge nurse? If it is a staff group decision, then what kind of conference, led by what person, should be required? At this time on the ward, some erratic new patients are admitted and a testing of the limits of staff control of the ward occurs. Several of the patients "escape" during this period, partly in order to test the authority of the staff, partly to test its cohesion. As the outbreaks of hostility flare and as new patients are gradually added to the present group, the patients are faced with a dilemma similar to the staff's. In essence, the solution worked out by each group is to find a nucleus of strength in the example of some of the stronger members. Individual members of the staff gain respect when it is discovered that their decisions, whether right or wrong, are not followed by catastrophes. No one is fired and none of the patients dies, or becomes a fugitive from the hospital. Three of the patients, Miss Bernard, Miss Serena and Mrs. Cooper, form the nucleus of a subgroup which is a respected, stable example of close cooperation among individuals of separate strength.

Period III. The third period in the chronology of the ward's infancy lasts until December 15. As individual members of the staff begin to develop a stronger sense of self-respect, their decision making becomes increasingly autonomous. The old coalition of liberals now wants to legislate new freedoms such as an open-door policy, a freer choice of bedtimes and street clothes rather than uniforms for the nurses. Mr. Gordon, the Social Worker, is a key stabilizing figure and at this time shifts slightly toward the liberal position. Staff members develop a sense of "democratic participation." Dr. Isaacson, preoccupied with the ward's financial problems, is also busy implementing a liaison service for the rest of the hospital. It becomes apparent that it will be necessary to admit and treat more patients in order to survive economically.

The "escape" of some patients further threatens the ward's potential to survive. One of the patients who "escapes" is a close relative of an influential founder of the hospital. Dr. Isaacson is under increasing external pressure and on one occasion is embarrassed when an event occurs on the ward about which he remains uninformed and hence unable to transmit particulars to the concerned family. Thus, he must translate the external pressures back to the ward and regain close control. This is documented in a series of memos issued at the end of November. They state that uniforms are to be worn, that relations between patients and staff members are to use the formal designation of surnames, that Dr. Isaacson himself is to be informed of immediate problems. Thus the chain of command is reiterated. Dr. Schwartz, who has recently come from the municipal hospital as a part-time Assistant Director,[1] or Miss Conrad, the Head Nurse, is to be notified if Dr. Isaacson is unavailable. During the same period Miss Spodney and another "older" nurse are hired, adding a further note of structure to the staff.

Individual staff members are somewhat resentful of the reassertion of leadership at first, but because they feel a common bond, they are able to resolve their difficulties by working hard together. The patients undergo an intense group experience at their own level. Suicidal feelings are expressed openly within the group. Mrs. Cooper, one of the triumvirate of "in-group" patients, is discharged during this period and her absence activates feelings of loss which are an important element in the pathology of many patients. The common experience of loss and the understanding of one another's feelings produce a resolution of suicidal ideas through the security of common bonds.

---

[1] The formal designation of Assistant Director is not proffered until nearly a year later.

Period IV. The next period, encompassing Christmas, lasts through February. It is a time when the ward census rises rapidly. Dr. Isaacson's close attention becomes diluted and Dr. Schwartz must now implement his authority. Under the increasing strain of work many of the preceding resolutions are weakened. Mr. Gordon's "Countertransference Workshop" with the nurses becomes a focus of difficulty. Rebellious attitudes within the nursing staff are expressed openly and Miss Conrad feels that the workshop exacerbates the tension. The workshop, begun as an exercise in understanding feelings about patients, threatens to aggravate the tendency to act out hostile feelings. Symptomatic of the rebellious spirit, a Christmas party is held on the ward which is attended by some outside guests and serves as an occasion for intermingling of staff and patients under semisocial circumstances. The party evades the attention and control of the November edicts. Miss Serena meets her future husband at this party, a secret to which only a few staff members are privy.

During this period the patients suddenly allow a new patient, Mr. Novick, to take over as their leader. In the murals, for instance, the others become ancillary contributors to Mr. Novick's artistic production. Mr. Novick provides a source of preoccupation for both the patients and the staff. He exercises the seductive charm of a bad but precocious boy, which thoroughly disarms the staff. The staff does not know how to deal with him and is distressed with his therapist, Dr. Augress. Dr. Augress, an original member of Group A, has been handling most of Dr. Isaacson's private patients and he has become linked in symbolic ways with Dr. Isaacson. The staff attempts to take advantage of Dr. Isaacson's distraction by usurping his decision-making power. However, unable to effect real changes through rebellion, the staff and patients both turn to a displacement figure, a "scapegoat." This figure serves to focus the unsuccessful aggressive feelings and allows symbolic gratification of these angry strivings.

Period V. The succeeding period of February and March marks the beginning of disintegration in the group's structure. The scapegoat leaders are subjected to real punishment during this time. Dr. Schwartz is experienced as imposing Dr. Isaacson's authority without a genuine basis for doing so. Mr. Novick's infantile helplessness becomes progressively more obvious. The nursing rebellion becomes more pronounced despite the discontinuation of Mr. Gordon's "Countertransference Workshop." Miss Marsh finds herself at the head of the insurgency group. Miss Conrad, who has experienced increasing weakness, is actually becoming physically ill and as of March 1 she must take a leave of absence of several months duration.

Another patient figure emerges as a convenient focus and displacement figure for many feelings. Mrs. Hecht, an editor of psychiatric books, and a patient of Dr. Schwartz, becomes anorectic while on the ward. She is finally "saved" through the efforts of the staff, all of whom take turns in tube feeding her. During this period the patients are preoccupied with sadistic feelings and again and again use Mr. Novick as a target. He is elevated to leadership, deposed, resurrected and killed anew. Leading the carnage is a subgroup of Dr. Lukens' patients. Each mural session becomes a symbolic castration of Mr. Novick and finally of Dr. Lukens. Mr. Phillips, a successful but acutely depressed patient of Dr. Lukens, surreptitiously assumes the leadership, which he steals from Mr. Novick, and for a time even members of the staff look to him for guidance. As his discharge approaches at the end of this period, the staff and patients reunite once again as each person becomes simultaneously a protective leader and a victim. All members of staff "save" Mrs. Hecht, and through her Dr. Schwartz, from their own aggression. Each member of the patient group rescues Mr. Novick, and through him Drs. Augress and Lukens, from their own aggression. They all fear retribution for their sadism and the consequences of having no leader.

Period VI. The sixth period encompasses April and May. Miss Marsh is now Head Nurse Designate in Miss Conrad's absence and finds it rough sailing. Her brand of individual response to the patients, while exemplary, does not organize the nursing staff sufficiently. Now that the "rebellion" has "succeeded," the nurses find themselves in a kind of void. Each element of the staff is now an island of authority unto itself; each doctor with his coterie of patients constitutes a separate fragment. In the midst of this disorganization, Mr. Foley, is admitted. Not only does he have the appearance of a cultist, hippy leader who is unable to restrain his aggressive outbursts, but he is a close relative of a chief hospital administrator. He is assigned to Dr. Augress. It becomes apparent that control can not be exerted over this new patient. He comes and goes as he pleases. On one occasion when he has been confined to the tiny seclusion room he breaks the plaster from the walls and ceiling. The patients, feeling unprotected, abandon themselves to their image of an avenging wraith. The composition of the patient group has become more psychotic than it has ever been. The murals are now filled with fantasies of self-destruction and annihilation. The structure undergoes psychotic fragmentation as regressive fantasies emerge. The resolution of this period involves an abandonment of reality.

Period VII. During the next period, lasting until the end of June, Mr. Foley is temporarily discharged. The nursing staff turns in fascination to a new figure, Miss Salvatore.

Miss Salvatore seems to embody all the elements of sweetness and competence of the ideal nurse. In short order she is appointed to be Miss Marsh's assistant and now the members of the nursing staff are unified as they work to please her. Two other "maternal" figures appear on the scene at this time. One sits at a desk by the entrance and becomes a sympathetic listener to the adolescent patients on the ward. They congregate about her desk which is located just outside the music room. Rock enchantment now issues from the music room for most of the day. A new secretary has been employed to take over the reorganization of financial matters. Dr. Isaacson is concerned with the laxity in billing which has heretofore prevailed. Patients now are more passive, somehow younger in spirit, and the sweet, pungent odor of cannabis has been noticed more than once by certain staff members. Miss Allen, a bright adolescent girl, assumes a role among the patients parallel to Miss Salvatore's role among the staff. She maintains the "psychedelic" atmosphere first imposed on the ward by Mr. Foley. However, as the time for Miss Allen's discharge approaches and as Miss Salvatore, who is now indispensable, also prepares to leave the ward, to be married, the group is left once again to grope regressively. In the mural, images of birth and early maternal faces point toward the resolution of this period.

Period VIII. The final period of the year leads to the mass exodus of staff for vacations. Although everyone is fatigued, some will remain. An aura of sadness permeates the group, but there is a nascent hope emerging for the future as well. Miss Conrad will be returning and Dr. Isaacson is not leaving for his vacation during the month of August as many of the staff will do. Miss Salvatore is gone and among the patients several discharges have occurred, including Miss Allen. The patients who must remain during the summer doldrums are by and large those who are too sick to mobilize themselves.

Now faced with the impending reality of massive loss of objects and with their own internal structures decimated, patients as well as staff turn inward to find the deepest vestiges of strength still remaining. For members of staff, this is the hope for total relaxation on their vacations and the anticipation of a future with renewed order. For the patients, Ward 12-N, Theodore Herzl Hospital becomes a shelter beyond the auspices of any human being. In the mural sessions the patients finally depict themselves as a sad band of nomads searching the arid reaches of their common past for vestiges of life. This is the bare bones, as it were, of the staff and patients coming together and making of themselves an institutional group. These fragmented allusions to the ward's history are perhaps no more than the skeletal remains of some unknown beast of a bygone era. Just as the caveman left sketches that spoke of his world, so have the patients created in their group mural a testament to their world. By taking the year's progress in eight consecutive periods and comparing these periods to the information derived from the murals, a reconstruction of the ward's reality emerges.

Stages

When the authors sit down with the 50 murals and the corresponding protocols describing the transactions of each mural session, they decide to evaluate the data in the following way. Each mural is considered separately in order to determine the most prominent theme which it expresses. First, a continuity emerges between the group's expression one week and the expression in the week to follow. It appears that the group grapples with one problem for a period of time and then gradually becomes concerned with another. As the 50 murals are surveyed, it becomes apparent that they naturally classify themselves into different types. These types are:

1. Reality-bound mural
2. Mural which states the group's problem in a more or less disguised form
3. Mural of anxiety, flight and defense
4. Mural dealing topographically with the unconscious
5. Mural which recombines the recent symbols in restitutive terms
6. Mural of resolution and return to reality

Once this sequence of stages is identified, it becomes apparent that there is an invariant order from stages one through six and that the sequence of these stages repeats with each new problem in reality. For instance, a mural with the classical land/water division depicting the unconscious will never precede a mural of anxiety and flight. With the analysis of the mural sequence taken this far, it is natural to see the group's problem-solving task as related to the reality conditions which prevailed on the ward. By classifying each period according to the problem facing the group and its resolution, one notes further internal consistency (see Charts 2 and 3.) Each mural of resolution accords logically with the precursor mural which states the group's problem. Viewed in this way, a continuous story of the group's inner life emerges. In Chart 2 the first four phases of the ward's life are elaborated in respect to each mural and its place in the sequence.

In a sense, the patient group is confronted with a problem the solution to which is arrived at through a natural creative process. The group's creative method is no different from that which is described by creative men. A period of mulling something over yields to a feeling that the problem is insoluble, and that it must be avoided; subsequently there is a sense of internal unconscious work followed by inspired representation and elaboration of a solution. Conceivably, the fact that the group undergoes this process without any sense of long-range goal orientation indicates that it is participating in a natural and general phenomenon. By studying each mural of a particular stage in this creative process, it becomes possible to detail the work of that stage.

Stage I: Reality. The very first mural called "House" is merely a description of the here and now. The patients simply present a cross-section of the ward's living space. By sticking to the bare outlines of their external reality, they avoid any mutual confrontation. Somehow they are to form a group, but the first consideration is the conditions under which a group will be formed.

At the beginning of the second sequence the patients, having formed a group, are now confronted with newly arrived patients. The group structure is about to be threatened by hostility from within and by having to accommodate its living space to new people. The initial mural of this sequence is entitled "Floor Plan of a House" (# 9).[2] The resolution mural of sequence three and the reality mural of sequence four are combined in the mural of December 8 called "Sightseeing in Metropolis" (#18). In this mural the patients are portrayed as a group of people standing on a public plaza.

In a way, the patients' presentation of reality in the murals is inconsistent with the concept of "art." When the mural portrays reality there is little distinction between form and content. Of course no picture, not even a photograph, can be entirely representative of perceptual reality. Even a floor plan begins to delete some of reality's content and to substitute a symbolic form. However,

---

[2] We are missing the mural protocol of November 3, 1966, which corresponds to the beginning of the third sequence. This is the mural that should consist of a reality depiction. The title "Heaven and Hell" (#14) and the pictorial contents suggest that, once again, the ward is the locale.

CHART 2

GROUP MURAL SEQUENTIAL CHART

SEQUENCE I: How can staff resolve liberal vs. conservative approach to create a therapeutic ward?

Date	Title	Theme	Creative Stage	Group Structure or Task
8/4/66	A House	How to hide	Reality	There is no group
8/11/66	Circus	Object hunger	Statement	How to trust each other to form group
8/18/66	An Auto Trip	Danger of satisfactions	Defensive	To symbolize satisfaction while keeping separate
8/25/66	Underwater Scene	Mutual aggression	Unconscious	Relationship through a serene denial of aggression
9/1/66	Abstract	How to control anger	Unconscious/ Recombination	Restructuring group to avoid anger
9/8/66	A Home	Wish for fusion	Recombination/ Resolution	Division into complementary camps
9/15/66	Metropolis	Sharing	Resolution	Group equality and cohesion
9/22/66	Farm Scene	Multiple Satisfaction	Resolution/ Reality	Symbiotic group

SEQUENCE II: Staff role differentiation while avoiding criticism

Date	Title	Theme	Creative Stage	Group Structure or Task
9/29/66	Floor Plan of a House	Fear of Disintegration	Reality	How to prevent group disintegration with new patients
10/6/66	Forest Fire A Planet	Flight from Hostility	Statement/ Defensive	Group disintegration as individuals flee hostility
10/13/66	A Country Place	How to prevent mutual infringement	Defensive	Part integrated, part disintegrated group
10/20/66	Land & Water	Fear of each other	Unconscious	Small group formation for protection
10/26/66	Museum	Individuation	Recombination/ Resolution	Oldest subgroup shows way to individuated cooperation

SEQUENCE III: Staff internalizes director's values although he is unavailable

Date	Title	Theme	Creative Stage	Group Structure or Task
11/10/66	Zoo	Irritated withdrawal	Statement	How can group survive loss of key members
11/17/66	Geometric Forms	Separateness	Defensive	Group members withdraw from each other
12/1/66	3000 A.D.	Identification with lost object	Unconscious/ Recombination	Internalization of each other

Date	Sightseeing in	...protection from	Resolution/ Reality	
12/8/66	Metropolis	Protection from suicide		Forming intrapsychic protection of each other, even from inner hurt
SEQUENCE IV: New leader sparks hard work while rebellion flares				
12/15/66	Jungle	Ambivalent interactions	Statement	How can group survive its own aggression as a body
12/22/66	Cape Cod	Denial of aggression (no protocol)	Defensive	Group subservience to powerful male projection
1/5/67	Outer Space	Suppression of aggression	Defensive	Old subgroup leaves, new is united with Novick
1/12/67	Country Scene	Rebellion against leader	Unconscious	Group turns its aggression to Novick
1/19/67	Fishing Village	Murder of leader	Recombination/ Resolution	New group united in aggression to scapegoat new leader
1/26/67	Carnival			

CHART 3

SUMMARY OF GROUP'S STRUCTURAL DEVELOPMENT AS DERIVED FROM MURAL

Sequence	Statement of problem	Resolution
I. 8/4/66 to 9/22/66	How to trust each other to form a group	Form a diffuse equal group with one division
II. 9/29/66 to 10/26/66	How to prevent group disintegration with new patients	The oldest subgroup shows the way to individuated cooperation
III. 11/10/66 to 12/8/66	How can group survive loss of key members	Protect each other, even from inner hurt
IV. 12/15/66 to 1/26/67	How can the group survive its own aggression without a leader	Elevate a new leader and scapegoat him
V. 2/2/67 to 3/20/67	How can the group survive if it kills its leader (symbolically)	Everyone becomes the leader by eating him
VI. 3/30/67 to 4/20/67	How can the guilty, leaderless group respond to an attack	By allowing itself to be overwhelmed and victimized
VII.A. 4/27/67 to 6/1/67	How can the group find itself again	By being reborn and letting one member portray mother
B. to 6/28/67	How can the group face the loss of that mother	By hating her image
VIII. 6/28/67 to 8/2/67	How can the group survive such inner hostility	By projecting archaic good-mother images onto the institution

the murals which initiate the sequences are closest to the actual situation on the ward. The group's increased concern with reality is analogous to an individual's increased self-consciousness when a significant problem is just emerging. There is also an increased consciousness and preoccupation with the mural itself, even the cardboard in this stage.

Stage 2: Statement. The second stage of a sequence consists of making a statement about a problem which the group faces. In "Circus" (#2) of the first sequence the patients want to form a group in which members give satisfaction to one another and the problem is how to trust one another enough to accomplish this. In the statement murals of the subsequent three sequences, the group, having already been formed, faces the problem of ensuring its survival. The murals of statement often use animal forms to depict yet simultaneously disguise the identity of each person. Note the animals in "Circus" (#2) of sequence one, in "A Planet" (#10B) of sequence two, in "Zoo" (#15) of sequence three, in "Jungle" (#19) of sequence four, "Zoo" (#33) of sequence six and "Jungle" (#38) of sequence seven. In the "Circus" (#2) mural of sequence one, the animals are portrayed in their lack of relationship, all facing the same direction, looking for a strong ringmaster. There is as yet no sense of relationship among the individual animals. "A Planet" (#10B) of sequence two shows the animals hiding from each other as the feared disintegration of the group is depicted. By presenting themselves in a disguised version the patients begin a process of symbolization. As the content of their reality is further separated from its form, the form becomes a mental representation. The structural relationship between members of the group is maintained as their identity becomes disguised and symbolized. In this way it is possible to state relationships which would be too threatening otherwise. Reducing their identity to symbols also allows them to begin to facilitate trial solutions to their mutual problems. The mural lends itself to enhancing the symbolization process, and to reducing reality to a form which accords more closely with mental structures.

Stage 3: Defense. The defense stage is one in which the elements of movement or flight are stressed. For instance, in the first sequence the mural "An Auto Trip" (#3) suggests a movement farther away from the scene of the ward's reality. Although some satisfactions are portrayed along the route, the dangers of obtaining the satisfactions are emphasized. Frequently the defense stage shows the fears of the patients as coming to pass. In the sixth sequence the title of the mural is "End of the World" (#34). The group has the problem in this sequence of maintaining itself without a leader, but it portrays the rampant destruction which it fears. It is as if the patients say, "If it's going to happen we will make it happen." In sequence eight the mural of the defense stage is entitled "Anxiety" (#46). Here the patients are in the process of undergoing a significant regression. Frequently the defense mural takes the escapist form of creating a pleasant scene. Thus in sequence two, "A Country Place" (#11) has been rendered. In sequence four "Cape Cod" (#20) and "Country Scene" (#22) are the pleasant places of denial. In sequence six a long period of three successive defense murals passes from "Winter Scene" (#26) to "Big Rock Candy Mountain" (#27) and finally moves more actively in "Mobiles" (#28). The more regressed group in sequence seven chooses "Fairyland" (#39) and "Transylvania" (#40) as its refuge from reality. The length of involvement in this stage of the sequence varies between one and three weeks. Usually at least two weeks are necessary before the group continues to move to the actual place of the unconscious. In this stage the threatening representations of reality are bound to mental structures which are repressed or otherwise dealt with defensively.

Stage 4: Unconscious. It is strange to think of the unconscious as a place, yet the most striking regularity to emerge in this process is the expression of the unconscious in terms of setting. In sequence one it is "Underwater Scene" (#4); in sequence two, "Land and Water" (#12); in sequence three "3,000 AD" (#17) (in which a large area of water appears); sequence four, "Fishing Village (#23); sequence five, "A Beautiful Underwater Scene" (#29); sequence six, "Emotions" (#35); sequence seven "Dreams" (#41), alternatively entitled, "Oceans"; sequence eight, "An Island" (#47).

By the use of water and a land/water division it is possible to portray a deep place of feelings in relation to a symbolic form of reality. This stage provides the inspiration for forming a solution to the group's problem. It is here in the unconscious realm that large shifts of energy can occur. In each sequence the problem faced by the group stems from a difficulty in dealing with hostility. The solution which is sought is always one involving a structural change within the group. This must come about through a reorganization of the aggressive forces within the group. It is in the unconscious stage that such a reorganization occurs.

The serenity of "Underwater Scene" (#4) of the first sequence reacts against the aggressive threat feared by all group members. A more or less uniform field is created underwater where each underwater thing is in a distant but equal relationship to each other thing. A kind of territorial imperative is set up. In the second sequence's "Land and Water" (#12) the contributions are clustered into subgroups. Conceivably the means of expressing aggressive drives is transferred from the whole group to a subgroup. In the third sequence, "3,000 AD" (#17), the work of this stage appears to be a kind of infusion of energy into the images of other group members until their significance approaches that of self-images. In "Fishing Village" (#23) of sequence four a fascinating shift occurs such that the group's entire means of aggressive discharge is transferred to the person of Mr. Novick. The energy transformations of the latter four periods will be taken up in a later section. Essentially, this is a stage of communication between drive and symbol, inner and outer. The interface between inner and outer self is opened, and the identification is created.

Stage 5: Recombination. In this sometimes transient stage the transformations which have been effected in the unconscious stage are given a symbolic form which will allow reality to be restitutively approached once more. There is a strong desire to reengage reality, attended by a feeling of effective and bountiful energy. In "A Home" (#6) of sequence one, two homes are actually drawn. These give form to the two large group sectors which can effectively counterbalance the forces in each other. This mural reminds us of the two camps, "Liberal" and "Conservative," into which the staff ordered itself.

In the second sequence, "Museum" (#13), which also serves as a mural of resolution, reveals the formation of subgroups which insure their own survival, if not that of the whole group. Thus the redistribution of attachments which was noted finds an equivalent form for becoming meaningful in reality.

In the third sequence "3,000 AD" (#17) serves as a

mural of the recombination stage as well as the unconscious stage. In this mural an intrapsychic group is
created in the mind of each group member so that the
loss of real members does not disrupt the cohesiveness of
the mental image of the group. If the image of other
group members is on a par with the self-image, then each
member's mental image of the group is capable of absorbing a great deal of hostility, without loss of cohesion.

In "Carnival" (#24) of the fourth sequence, the aggression is all turned onto Mr. Novick, who in the mind
of each group member, now serves in the role of leader. Since he has become the internal representative of
the group his image is available to absorb much of the
aggressive drive that is generated in the various group
members.

Stage 6: Resolution. In the final stage of resolution the
newly structured solution is brought into contact with
reality. At this point, insofar as the resolution expresses
the new form of the group, it becomes vulnerable to
change or destruction.

In sequence one both "Metropolis" (#7) and "Farm
Scene" (#8) contain images of shared satisfaction un-
threatened by mutual hostility. In the "Museum" (#13)
mural of sequence two each member of the major subgroup is framed as an individual on the museum wall.
In "Sightseeing in Metropolis" (#18) of sequence three
the patients constantly protect one another from suicidal
impulses. In "Carnival" (#24) of sequence four the
aggression is turned definitively onto the leader. Chart 3
indicates the logical continuity between a problem, its
resolution and the succeeding problem. Insofar as these
stages repeat themselves in an invariant order, and to the
extent that in their entirety they form a meaningful
movement from problem to resolution, the question

arises as to the nature of the general phenomenon which underlies this process. If this is the creative method, then something is being created; that is, something is being created against the force of aggression.

As one of its properties it lends structure to the group. We are suggesting that what has been created is a group self. It has come about via the mechanism of identification and is the work of identity creation.

3

THE WORK OF IDENTITY CREATION

Sequence I: Group Formation (8/4/66–9/22/66)

IN this chapter individual mural sessions will be reported in detail within the context of the ward's ongoing reality. By the time that patients are admitted, the staff of the Hospital Psychiatric Ward has aligned itself into two major segments, A and B. The alignment reflects their divergent approaches to potential patient hostility. Looking back on this time, Group A says:

Their (B's) expectations were that we (A) would be conservative, authoritarian and rigid.

They (B) were sloppy.

They (B) wanted patients that they had liked at the Municipal Hospital: young, intelligent, verbal, not too sick.

They (B) were permissive—afraid to promote the expression of anger by restrictions, because they were afraid of their own aggressiveness. Group B says:

They (A) wanted to care for everyone.

They (A) wanted a suicide-proof unit.

They (A) would let you do anything you wanted, but mistakes were not allowed.

There was not enough support when people did make mistakes.

In August, 1966, when the Director is on vacation, Dr. Simon, his assistant, tries to launch patient government out of a series of ward meetings. A member of Group B comments later, "He wasn't successful because everyone knew he was going away." And everyone also knew that Dr. Isaacson would consider patient government premature.

Dr. Isaacson wears a white lab coat while working. He wants nurses to wear uniforms. His reason for this, in line with his liaison work, is that the "psychiatric unit be considered firmly a part of the whole hospital." His involvement with the unit activities forms a pattern of intense short-term involvement at times of crisis. For instance, after the first Assistant Director leaves he conducts daily rounds, but these are soon cut back to once a week, whereupon others take over.

Although classified with Group B, Mr. Gordon, the Psychiatric Social Worker, is also allied closely with both Dr. Isaacson and Dr. Schwartz. This alliance, as well as his role in meeting with the nursing staff in weekly "Countertransference Conferences" establishes him as a buffer. He is aware of the necessity to postpone the ideal of patient government in the service of a more immediate pragmatic end—a relatively serene therapeutic milieu. His extensive involvement with the ward also sees him leading patient groups and meeting with patients' families. He states, "The nurses were inexperienced and had an exaggerated concept of what can be done for people." He feels that part of the staff fears patient group formation. He agrees with Dr. Evans of Group B and Miss Conrad of Group A that overt hostility is forbidden: "We could tolerate anything except anger."

Given the prevailing attitude toward anger, the staff is faced with the task of incorporating it into a truly therapeutic community. How much supervision of patient activity will be required? No one knows what illness will be present, and Group A doesn't want the blame for failure to foresee and control the untoward consequences of patient destructiveness. Group B wants to forbid any activity which would seriously menace an environment in which freedom would be the basis for better understanding. There is a feeling of excitement as discussions are held and decisions are made. Will regular cutlery be allowed; should it be counted? Shower rods are elevated. Will there be drapery cords? What will constitute contraband items? Will the ward door be locked? Will the nurses wear uniforms? There are problems in construction details. The furniture doesn't arrive in time. The allotted office for therapists is questioned and rearranged. From excitement grows uneasiness.

Uneasiness seems to permeate the unit from the date of the first admission. The first six patients are "nice patients." The only male has his own special nurse. Three stay a short time. Three others are suicidal women: Miss Bernard, Mrs. Cooper and Miss Serena. They become friends despite varied backgrounds.

Nursing is well staffed, actually overstaffed for the first month's number of admissions. There is only one male member of the nursing staff. "They were of high calibre," comments Dr. Simon, "but inexperienced." They are young and new in the field of psychiatry. They are afraid to make mistakes and afraid of direct confrontations. They are self-conscious and awkward. Dr. Evans states, "The nurses were frightened by the verbal aggression of the intelligent, sophisticated, sarcastic, more educated, upper-class patient."

Mrs. Cooper is a sensitive but compulsive and depressed young middle-class mother. She had a need to prove her ability to be an organized wife and mother. On the ward she constantly presented herself to Miss Serena and Miss Bernard as one who could be relied upon.

Miss Bernard, a patient of Dr. Evans, is an intelligent, sophisticated, sometimes sarcastic, upper-class patient. Her father, with whom she identified, was an influential member of the Herzl Board of Directors. Despite the tragic circumstances leading to her admission, she was unable to acknowledge that she wanted and needed help. Her pattern of guarded interaction was such that she invariably waited for proof of acceptance before involving herself. This frustrated the young idealistic nurses. A random sample of her statements during her first two months on the ward includes: "The 'irrational' rules, such as no visitors for the first two weeks, should be broken!"; "What do nurses do if they don't like a patient?"; "It's not a therapeutic community, there is no communication between older and younger patients." The dynamic tone for patient and staff group formation arises out of such challenges.

One patient, Miss Serena, plays a major role in the murals and in the group's early formation. She participates in the first mural and is a regular contributor to the murals for the period of August 1966 to January 1967. Miss Serena was admitted under the auspices of Medicaid, when the ward's needs for patients was great. The staff wanted to determine whether a patient with a social background different from the upper middle-class private patient could benefit from the ward's milieu. Her presence on the ward comes to catalyze one of the polarizations of the staff. The aides identify with her as the underdog. They even secretly bring her forbidden ham sandwiches. She is a bright and chipper, sexy child-woman who excels in drawing people into an intense relationship with her. The relationships often are short-lived as she easily senses any semblance of rejection and becomes cold. She made a dramatic suicide gesture six months before admission, hanging by her finger tips from a window ledge. Unable to maintain her grasp, she dropped three stories, breaking her pelvis and both legs. The depression was precipitated by a threat to the symbiotic relationship that she had maintained with a half-sister. The half-sister had shown a covert preference for her own full sister. Miss Serena ruminates about suicide once again at the time of her admission to 12-N. It becomes clear early in her therapy that she is constantly reproducing in her life the intense, symbiotic relationship that she had experienced with the aunt who raised her.

She lived, in poverty, with her mother in a metropolis until the latter died when she was three. Thereafter, she lived with her father until she was five upon which she went to live with an elderly aunt in the rural mountains of Puerto Rico. She constantly wanted to run away, but feared that such a hostile act would actually kill her aunt. When she would return after brief junkets, her aunt would beat her "for her own good." When she was 16 her aunt died. Miss Serena felt immensely guilty about the aunt's death and she experienced an immediate depression in which she stopped eating and felt in her dreams that the aunt was calling her to death to join her. These dreams recurred even until the time of her admission to 12-N.

The brunt of her psychotherapy was to allow the symbiosis to form again with the therapist and to work it through from the standpoint of its being unrealistic and self-destructive. The manner in which she transfers feeling from the earlier relationship with the aunt to the therapist was pointed out repeatedly. She developed a fear of monsters at those points the meaning of which was explained to her in terms of her own murderous feelings toward the aunt and toward the therapist.

Murals

The structure formation in the ward group resulting

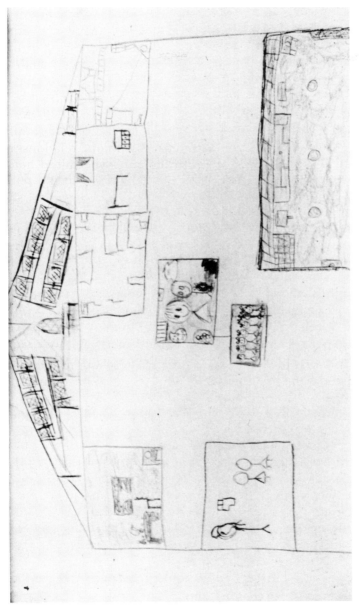

Sequence I: Group Formation. Stage 1: Reality. "HOUSE," August 4, 1966, Mural #1.

from a process of overcoming mutual aggressions finds a parallel in Miss Serena's development. In the first mural on August 4 the theme is the hospital itself. The patients are faced with the task of forming a group, specifically a mural group, despite the mistrust which they feel for one another and for the staff inasmuch as they are strangers to each other. By sticking to the here and now the patients can keep their feelings and their identities separate from one another. This is a very self-conscious reality-bound mural in which the patients do not reveal themselves easily. They are afraid of making a mistake and there is no resort to symbolism. It is felt to be unsafe to portray emotion. This is seen in the thematic constriction, in the black unrevealing colors, in the stick figures and in the overall reluctance to participate.

The description of the initial mural meeting will try to recreate the mood, atmosphere and some of the essential content: One begins by trying to imagine the anxiety a person might feel walking into a room to which he has been directed with "It's time to go," finding a semicircle of chairs and a person seated behind the chairs awaiting him with watchful eyes. How frightening it must be for one who has always been last, now to be the first to arrive in this foreboding setting, seemingly at the mercy of the one behind the chairs with the pencil and the paper and the ever-watchful eyes observing every move, seeing every tremor, every bead of sweat. And the huge gray board, overwhelming in its size, awesome in its grayness, portentous in its emptiness. How painful to bend one's body into a chair, to be trapped there for God knows how long, for as long as the one behind the chairs wants him there. This is the way it may be for the first patient who enters the room to begin what is to become the first mural group of ward 12-N.

In this case, the first person to be encountered behind the semicircle of chairs is one of the nurses, Miss Shaw, who has been asked by Mr. Blackman to record the first session, Mural #1, 8/4/66.

Mr. Blackman enters a moment after the patients he was out trying to motivate have assembled. He enters to find them awaiting him in complete silence, and he remarks on the quietness of the room.

Then, as should be a matter of routine procedure for those unfamiliar with the mural and its purpose in this setting, he explains the whys and wherefores, being careful to add a note on the necessity for keeping a record of what is done and how. This is, of course, to explain Miss Shaw's function and her presence in the room. Time is also given to an introduction of the medium to be used and an orientation to the overall structure as it relates to the three mural stages.

The increase in the clicking mouth movements of Mrs. Grier in response to the art therapist's call for group cooperation can be said to have expressed the anxiety of the other patients and staff, as well as her own.

Mrs. Grier was the first admission to Ward 12-N and for several days had been the sole recipient of all the concern and attention of an impatient staff of nurses, doctors, aides and activity therapists, who had done and redone to the point of boredom the task of "setting things up" in preparation for treatment of the new arrivals. She is a pleasant, passive, elderly woman, who is unable to cope with her aging husband's childish demands as they grow senile together.

Mrs. Grier, being the first arrival, would naturally resent the "intrusion" of other patients with whom she must now share the staff's attention, although prior to their coming she often expressed her loneliness and displeasure at being the only patient "rattling around" on the ward. She had to suffer the attenuation of her status as the first patient to arrive on the unit and give way to the distinctions of other patients: Mr. Rappaport, the only male; Miss Serena, the only Afro-Latin, etc. They had to be given way to whether or not she respected the fact that these distinctions (ethnic, sexual, or whatever) hold a great deal of attraction for staff on both professional and emotional levels. One readily imagines how she must feel now, being asked by the art therapist and other members of staff to form a group with these "interlopers," to cooperate with them, to share with them the hard task of attempting to build a therapeutic community. One could say about the significance of Mrs. Grier's response, "She isn't just clicking her teeth."

1. Theme Selection. The group's first suggestion that houses will be the theme of the mural is most significant in that it also suggests a useful screen behind which the members of this pioneer group can conceal the telling of their feelings regarding their new environment, themselves and each other. This new environment, this hospital, this Ward 12-N is to be the real theme. It is first offered symbolically by Mrs. Cooper in the guise of "houses." Her second suggestion, "Let's draw the hospital," is reacted to like the dreaded opening of a Pandora's box by Miss Serena who, quickly but not too securely, slams it shut.

The "hospital" is a difficult subject for them to talk about. It is upsetting enough to have to be there, not to mention all the unpleasant thoughts and feelings associated with the experience. Except for the quiet interaction between Misses Serena and Hirsh, who sit together at one end, that semicircle of people presents a picture of profound depression, as exemplified by the following recorded statements: "Miss Kurtz sits, before the group starts, with arms folded tightly and with an angry look on her face. Mr. Rappaport taps his foot so that sound is noticeable. The rest of the group remains silent, staring blankly ahead. Mr. Rappaport begins breathing deeply and loudly and sits with his eyes closed, his head bowed down." Feelings of resentment, envy, and their by-product, hostility, are expressed, for example, by Miss Kurtz who says, "You younger people have better aptitude than older people. You can start and then we older people can kill it." Such a statement points to real feelings of alienation and distrust, prompting Mrs. Cooper to suggest the "hospital" theme.

Although in referring to the patients the term "group" has been introduced, it should be noted that at this point neither a viable group structure nor the ensuing community has been formed. Awareness of this fact sharpens the focus upon each patient's difficult struggle to make and to find the mutual commitment of trust essential to community development.

Miss Serena's objection to the obvious "hospital" theme may be seen as an expression of the unspoken anxiety of the other patients in the room. This being the case, one feels justified in speculating that her open objection and their silent agreement with that objection are the first indications of movement toward a collective awareness of the vulnerability of "souls" in isolation. This collective awareness may thus be seen as the germination of the process through which they will eventually achieve protective group formation. One may want to inquire at this point as to the nature of that which accounts for the patients' shared sense of vulnerability and their sympathetic need of protection.

Several factors may be drawn upon to account for their feelings of vulnerability:

1. No matter how many hospitalizations may have preceded the current one, this is a relatively new and experimental setting.

2. Although they are virtually strangers to each other,

the patients are being asked to share in a communal environment not of their design.

3. They are being summarily requested to enter into a situation with which they are unacquainted, with people they hardly know, and there to submit to graphic self-exposure.

4. Those doing the asking, the staff who is to care for them and provide for them the models of emotional stability, rationality and mental health, are themselves having difficulty resolving problems of disagreement regarding the relative values of the liberal versus the conservative approaches to the creation of a therapeutic community.

The patients are in this place, "inside," not because they want to be but because they have to be. They are here because they were brought here, sent here or wandered in on their own to take refuge from the world. The "hospital," and all it implies, is indeed a difficult subject to discuss at this time. No one is really ready to talk about his feelings quite that openly just yet. On that, each one can agree and in that unspoken agreement a group begins to form. And so they all agree to call their first mural a "house."

2. *The Mural.* "Mrs. Cooper suggested that Miss Serena initiate the drawing." Mrs. Cooper: young, attractive wife, mother, protagonist d'entente, leader of the struggle to form a group, drawn out by her own compelling need to become a whole person. Perhaps if she can accomplish something here, if she can be the effective leader, successful at pulling together the fragments in this "house," the result may be a self-orientation which might lead to some success at putting her own house in order.

"Miss Serena walked over to the box, picked up the black pastel and immediately started drawing in black—first the roof and then the walls. She explained as she drew, what she was drawing. Then moving to the upper left corner of the panel, she drew a box to represent the outlines of 'a small room.' She then drew the outlines of a sticklike table and flower pot."

Miss Serena, coming from an Afro-Latin background and a ghetto-based home, stands in marked contrast to the other patients. They are of middle and upper-middle class backgrounds and have come from homes and neighborhoods which tend to reflect their class differences. Though this racial and economic diversity exists, there are other significant bases upon which Miss Serena can identify equally and competitively. Like Mrs. Cooper, she is young, attractive and quite intelligent. Mrs. Cooper and Miss Serena could find considerable common ground on which to sympathetically relate.

Miss Serena seems disinclined at this juncture to oppose Mrs. Cooper's assumption of leadership. She is even tolerant of Miss Hirsh's suggestion that she "draw the outline of a room." One might have expected her to turn to her fellow patient and say, "If the outline of a room is what you want, get up and draw it yourself." Something in her eyes suggests that she will, but she doesn't.

Miss Hirsh, who is clearly contending for leadership, seeks presumably to maintain an air of aloofness and a position of autonomy. She cannot and will not at this moment bring herself to accept the direction of Mrs. Cooper, another patient, to whom she also need not respond from a position of class inequality. The two are fairly close in age. Miss Hirsh is an obese college student who is preparing to return to a distant college where she had experienced lonely desolation, self-contempt and urgent suicidal longings to return to a mother whose claim on her she had sought to deny.

Her suggestion to Miss Serena seems more like a rebuff to Mrs. Cooper's bid for leadership. Her opposi-

tion is further demonstrated when she goes to the panel
and tops Miss Serena's drawing with her "whole roof."
The message seems to be that she, Miss Hirsh, feels herself above any direction Mrs. Cooper might wish to provide.

Mrs. Cooper, apparently sensing this opposition, attempts to gain the support of the art therapist. Miss
Hirsh's subsequent attempt to involve Mr. Blackman in
her own behalf is her way of communicating her preference, at this time, for an authority rather than a peer-
directed group formation. She is not yet ready to be that
trusting of her fellow patients or involve herself in a
struggle with Mrs. Cooper and has called upon them for
directions merely to prove their inability to assume such
a task strictly on their own.

Mr. Blackman's refusal to intervene may be experienced by the patients as a gesture of encouragement to
"do their own thing." They are also mobilized to feel a
common bond of frustration, perhaps resentment, which
dulls their own personal frustration. This gives Mr.
Blackman an opportunity to become acquainted with
each patient's personal style, social aptitudes and levels
of frustration tolerance.

It is immediately after Mrs. Cooper's and Miss Hirsh's
efforts to involve the art therapist fail that the rallying
begins. More people become more active at the panel and
there is more verbal exchange, accompanied by laughter.
The laughter is an indication that tension release is occurring. The initial mood of potential hostility to one another is relieved by focusing it on Mr. Blackman. The
patients seem to reach the point of acceptance all at once
that they will be sharing this "House" for a considerable
amount of time.

Having accepted this fact, they decide to get acquainted through the creatively expressive means provided by the mural, where one can speak to his neigh-

bors indirectly when more direct communication becomes too difficult. Their silent agreement to make it on their own, indicates a tendency for independent growth which the liberal staff element would encourage. As they continue to speak through their various graphic symbols, a vivid picture of the conceptions of themselves in relation to their environment begins to emerge.

Miss Hirsh, who draws her "disconnected and haphazard lines," to represent bookshelves, may be stating in this way how insecure she really feels in her tower of intellectual isolation. Such are the feelings a young woman with her psychological orientation and professional aspirations for the future could well have as she stands upon the threshold of accepting her presence as a patient in a psychiatric ward with people whom she probably considers to be intellectually inferior to herself.

Who is Mrs. Cooper's smiling stick-figure girl, if not Mrs. Cooper herself? And at whom is she smiling, so evasively perhaps, if not at the lonely Miss Serena? To lend substance to this chance interpretation, it may help to consider each object's importance in terms of the order in which it is drawn.

Miss Serena comments on her first room which she drew several minutes earlier. She says that she "could not live alone." The comment is jokingly responded to by Miss Kurtz, who advises Miss Serena that she "could always have a ladder outside her window." This response might contain Miss Kurtz' own projections regarding loneliness, since she is a 35-year-old career woman who has wearied of her own distancing devices. But Mrs. Cooper, quickly rising, draws in the center of the panel a smiling stick-figure girl, in what later becomes her room, shared with her husband and child.

Miss Serena, after all, made visible the saddened countenance of loneliness for all to see. What that reality suggests relates directly to the reality suggested by Mrs.

Cooper's "Hospital," which elicited, as we may recall, a similar quick response from Miss Serena. That was during the stage of theme selection, a verbal stage which demands a direct verbal response to that which is accepted or opposed. Once the opportunity for graphic response is available, the form and quality of the response may vary considerably, yet we may see it as the same acceptance or denial of that which is being suggested.

The theme "House" can provide an effective screen for the real subject, "Hospital," behind which the patients can playfully relate to their feelings about being hospitalized and about being together. Who gets what room? How much more space is available for the people "outside"? Who will be desperately trying to get "inside"? These and more are matters of playful concern for children playing "house."

The recorder's report alludes to the drab, depressive atmosphere in which the game is played: "Up to this point all the individuals who have gotten up almost immediately chose the black pastel. No other colors have been introduced."

It is at this point that the bantering Miss Kurtz begins to, ever so lightly, verbally jostle Miss Serena. Are Miss Kurtz' "nicer curtains" a way of saying to Miss Serena, "I'm better defended against the pain of my loneliness than you are against yours?" Is the air conditioner in her room needed to cool her burning angers, fired by having been called upon to look at buried disappointments? And what about her bed? It will have two pillows and beneath her window there will, no doubt, be a good, sturdy ladder. Serena might be very much alone and lonely, but certainly not so the petulant Miss Kurtz.

Miss Serena's contribution to the mural is an open invitation to others to end loneliness through a kind of symbiosis. However, her remarks indicate that she can remain in her own comfortable room, finding a selfish haven of pleasure in narcissism if the others turn out to be unworthy of her trust.

Who should one get to know? Who should one dare to trust? When will the parting come? It's difficult and frightening to embark on new relationships, especially when the old ones haven't worked. But here the patients are working at getting acquainted: testing, trying, feeling their way. Ready to flinch, withdraw and hide. Ready to laugh, to force back a tear when some too familiar badinage is heard. A patient group is slowly being formed.

In the second mural, "Circus" (#2) the patients portray themselves as animals. This is a typical theme for new patients and for patients who are about to confront a problem. Circus, jungle or zoo themes recur regularly in the early stages of a new period on the ward. This type of mural is used to state the problem in a slightly disguised form. The group's reality has undergone a preliminary transformation into symbols and image. There is still a one-to-one accord between each patient and his production (animal). In the mural, each animal is separate from every other animal, sharing only in direction, as the movement through the hospital (big tent) is indicated. The ringmaster (chief of service, or the mural leader who puts them through their paces) is in a central position. It is important to note that Mr. Blackman, the art therapist, is absent and that Miss Callahan, the occupational therapist, is conducting the session in his place. The significance of this temporary change in terms of its effect upon the situation and the patients will become clearer later on. The ring of anonymous spectators portrays the staff watching the patients and probably the outsiders watching the ward. There is much loneliness and expression of hunger for each other in the big tent. Yet there is self-consciousness and fear of any action.

The need for a strong man (ringmaster) to help them out of this dilemma is expressed as in desperation the group tries, albeit in vain, to cast Mr. Rappaport with all his weakness, into this role. Mr. Rappaport is a bachelor whose characterological defenses of obsessiveness and isolation are failing as retirement approaches. In response to their overtures he announces that he had come merely to observe. Miss Kurtz, in her joking manner responded, "Oh, you're here to look in on us, but we can't look in on you"—a remark that seemed to tie him to authority figures both in and out of the mural setting, like Mr. Blackman, the art therapist, and Dr. Isaacson, the Chief of Service. Mrs. Cooper, then in a move to strengthen her bid for leadership, made during the previous mural, called upon the group to decide what to draw. Miss Serena, who we will recall was quick to respond in opposition to Mrs. Cooper's theme suggestion for the first mural, took a defensive position and suggested that everyone be allowed to do his own thing. To go back for a moment to Mrs. Cooper who had come into the room late, her specific statement was, "Have we decided what to draw?"—or put another way—"Have you made any decisions without me?" Miss Serena's response could then be interpreted as a resistance to any suggestion which might impose a structure of limitation upon her movements to find a relationship or relationships within the group based solely upon her needs and on her own terms.

The first animal symbol was suggested by Miss Hirsh, who thought that dinosaurs would be a good theme. This led immediately to the idea of a circus scene, an idea which seemed to gain the spontaneous approval of most of the group. Miss Hirsh, troubled by obesity, suggests a symbol for herself which also evokes the primitive past.

As the sequence develops, separation and aloneness becomes useful as a structural defense against the dangerous wishes for fusion and satisfaction in one another.

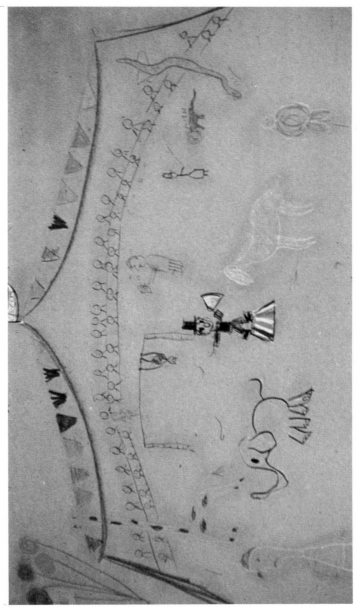

Sequence I: Group Formation. Stage 2: Statement. "CIRCUS," August 11, 1966, Mural #2.

Miss Kurtz suggests that someone begin by drawing a tent, "For us all to be in." Such a statement signifies their attempt in this place (the hospital) to get in touch with and express their feelings and all of the anxiety which drives them to play behind this unreal animal scene. For Miss Kurtz it is an attempt to be included within the group.

Mrs. Cooper "volunteers" to draw a large and "colorful" tent. As she draws, Mr. Rappaport, who has heretofore been reluctant to contribute either verbally or graphically without encouragement, offered an encouraging comment regarding Mrs. Cooper's efforts: "Very good," he said. He continues with such comments throughout the mural, usually in response to a drawing by Mrs. Cooper. His remarks are an effort to identify with the ringmaster, which he is at one point called upon to draw (and to be) but refuses. He is not just the only male in the group, but he is an elderly male as well. By asking him to "draw a ringmaster," Mrs. Cooper who senses that he is not really up to the task and therefore in no position to compete with her, seems to be saying, "We need a strong man to lead us." Mrs. Cooper asks, "Who'll draw a man holding balloons?" Mrs. Grier replies, "I will," then proceeds to draw a stick figure wearing a skirt.

Miss Bernard's "bland horse," a self-disguise as well as an object disguise, is even made use of in a put-down scene. The dialogue runs as follows:

Mrs. Cooper: "Is he (the horse/Mr. Rappaport) the type you have someone riding on?" or "Is he strong enough to carry the load?" or "Is he the strong man we need?"
Miss Bernard: "No! He's a bareback." or "He's spineless."
Mrs. Cooper: "Is it permittable to have someone stand—balance—on his back?" or "Can I ride—ridicule—him, focus on his weaknesses as a means of denying my own?"

Miss Bernard: "Yes." *or* "I'm with you; because if he's the spineless horse, then I can deny that it has anything to do with me."

At this point, Mrs. Cooper again tries to engage Mr. Rappaport in participating. As is predictable he refuses. His refusal draws forth a response from Miss Kurtz, who asks him, "When were you to the circus last?" To this Mr. Rappaport replies, "I don't remember." Miss Kurtz then continues her assault, this time as if to challenge him to verify his manhood. "You don't have nieces and nephews?" With obvious annoyance and deepening anger, Mr. Rappaport replies, "I have."

There is a relationship here between the mounting anxieties expressed in the group's annoyance with Mr. Rappaport for failing to stand the test and it's feeling "uptight" and unsupported; due to the absence of the real ringmaster or strongman, Mr. Blackman is that missing image in this self-revealing mural scene.

Directly following this episode with Mr. Rappaport, there is a shift engineered by Mrs. Cooper to Miss Serena, whom she encourages to contribute to the circus scene. The conflict of loneliness versus the danger of human contact, the conflict between secrecy and the desire to reveal everything are mirrored in Miss Serena's productions. Hers is the "lonely" but "courageous" lion and the "sexy" snake. Certainly the animal forms portray two deeper dimensions of her personality. She uses the symbolic disguises as a means of joining the group in its movement away from bare reality. The medium of the mural allows the group to vent its feelings in a way that is sufficiently disguised and symbolized so that its developing anxiety of expression is mastered. Statements such as the following express the group's concern with concealment and observation: "Does my monkey have ears? Your giraffe has to have bigger eyes." These are the words of Mrs. Cooper. How can one hear and see without being seen and heard? This seemed to be the question being articulated for the group at this point by Mrs. Cooper. The snake which was acceptable to Miss Serena for her own symbolic reasons, was really Mrs. Cooper's idea and it portrays Miss Serena, the only black member of the group, as sexy, dangerous and elusive. Miss Hirsh's observation about the snake as a leaping lizard projects her own symbol of annoyance, anger and anxiety in its place. The interchangeability of symbols is part of the movement toward creating a group. Her drawn image, the nonseeing giraffe, expresses yet another feeling and another need; the feeling of aloofness, of being above the group, and the need to deny (not to see) her affinity with its members as a patient in this hospital circus scene. Yet she had referred to the giraffe as a "diseased looking dinosaur," a remark which, at the time of its utterance, may have been intended to associate the symbol with her tormentor Mrs. Cooper, who was perhaps alluding to Miss Hirsh's moderate obesity with her, "You're going to draw an elephant," when Miss Hirsh stepped up to the panel. The animals chosen, relate to each person's pre-existing self-representation, and in this way self is being attached to images which convey the group's reality.

A degree of anxiety seemed to descend upon the group members at this moment, borne by the feeling that they are quarreling among themselves and running wild in the big tent. This was exacerbated by the fact that their leader, rather than appearing as the ringmaster, had impressed himself as a tightrope-walking monkey, so preoccupied with trying to maintain its own balance that it couldn't hear their pleas for order in the big tent. One must keep in mind that here the leader, ringmaster, strongman, mother, whatever one chooses to call him, refers symbolically to the group (mural) leader, the Art

Therapist, the Chief of Service, the doctor, and object images of the "grown-up" in each one's experience.

Miss Kurtz articulated the plea when she called for organization, but in a manner which suggested that she might be more capable than Mrs. Cooper at providing the group with the safety of orderly structure. It was her suggestion which led to the taking of turns, in order, as opposed to the random selecting and urging which preceded. Miss Serena, who was the first to go to the panel in this new order, began by apologizing to the group for having to use black. "I'm sorry I have to use black, I have to. I can't let it go."

Returning, for a moment, to an earlier point in this second mural session, Miss Kurtz' first graphic contribution to the "circus" was, she explained, "A little hole, and a kid looking through the hole who can't afford to go "inside." This is a familiar comic situation one sees portrayed many times in cartoons, plays, movies and other media which comment on the diversities of life. But her additional statement, "Everyone should see a circus by hook or by crook," beyond its self-revelatory quality may have been an allusion to Miss Serena, the one person in the group who (compared with the others) could least afford to come "inside." Miss Kurtz' words may have been an expression of her own awareness of this fact and her ambivalent feelings about having to share the circus scene with one of those kids who usually has to "look through the little hole." In this special environment "inside" was a microcosm of the larger environment, "outside," with its prejudices, its class distinctions and its current disturbing revolutionary black movement. Miss Serena's response is to courageously declare herself very much a part of the special scene, i.e., very much on the inside. After all, how much more important and respected can one be in this circus scene than as a lion,

albeit a lonely one. Always the lonely one, seeking to relate, wanting and yet fearing the intense closeness she
seemed to need. Perhaps she rationalized that her blackness and her poverty would lead in the end to rejection
and disappointment. "I'm sorry I have to use black,"
were her words; "I have to, I can't let it go." These words
could mean, "I'm sorry if my blackness alienates any of
you in this special white upper middle-class scene; but
I'm black and I can't be anything else, so you'll have to
take me or leave me just as I am." That is one interpretation and it has to do with a very real ethnocentric concern. There is, however, another shade to Miss Serena's
"black" which calls to mind her morbid dreams about
rejoining her dead aunt, her suicidal gesture and her
usual preoccupation with thoughts of death. The color
black may very often be seen as unrevealing, at least
from the patient's point of view; but in Miss Serena's
case, its repeated use is a most vivid symbolization of her
tormented life experience. She must hide herself from the
faceless spectators she draws in black; and one senses in
this expressionless treatment of the onlookers, her own
attempt to escape the stinging experiences of her days
and the monsters that stalk her nights. Other members of
the group share this need for concealment and escape
from reality, from each other, from their own aggression,
from night monsters, from the circus, from life. They had
dared to face all of these frightening aspects of their existence through their various animal guises, but the absence of a strong ringmaster made the task almost too
difficult to bear.

The third mural is "An Auto Trip" (#3). A heavily
outlined roadway is depicted, separating the travelers
from the myriad satisfactions that dot the environs. After
surveying signs for "Howard Johnson," "Hot Dogs," "Alcohol," "Eat Joe's" and "Try Schlitz," one patient says,
"This is one of the most fattening roads I've seen." "Dan-

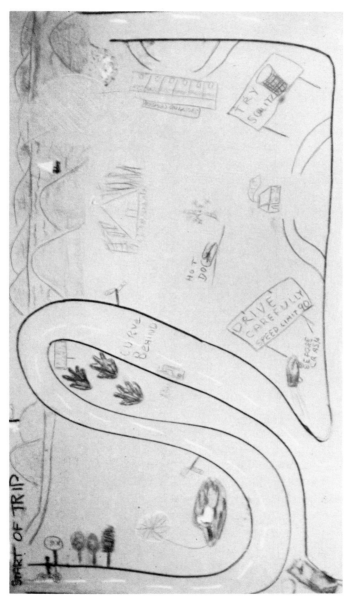

Sequence I: Group Formation. Stage 3: Defense. "AN AUTO TRIP," August 18, 1966, Mural #3.

ger ahead," "Stop," "Speed limit 90," indicates the dangers of such satisfactions. The movement away from reality and toward an unconscious confrontation with the designated problem is typical of this stage. It is a stage of defensiveness and transition. Certainly the content of the mural alludes to the patients' trip through the hospital and to the danger of tarrying too long like Theseus in the labyrinth. This aspect continues the theme of movement through the hospital begun when all of the animals faced the same way in the circus mural. The structure of the mural carries the sequence through the transition from statement to the unconscious. The personal identity themes of the "Circus" mural are now bearing the imprint of the group toward an unconscious confrontation with deeper sources of self-experience.

Miss Serena draws a stop sign first and then she draws a bar entitled, "Who Knows Bar" along the roadway. Subsequently, she draws mountains in the background. Evidently she is trying to stop her personal plunge into too much closeness. Closeness has resulted in self-annihilation in her previous experience. The "Who Knows Bar" may allude to a lack of inner identity, as well as to the question of who the other people really are. Certainly the mountains are the trademark of her youthful relationship with her aunt and it is to this location which her movements must ultimately take her. The mountains of her longing for her aunt represent the dangerous inner attractions for her. Miss Serena aptly expresses the group's need to defend itself against a symbiotic ultimately destructive fusion.

Although the group is very clear in stating its collective need of such defense, Miss Serena is the one who provides the most articulate symbols for its expression. Also, her immediate reaction to another patient's doorless house, "How do people get in and out?," clearly indicates her active involvement with the problem of entry into

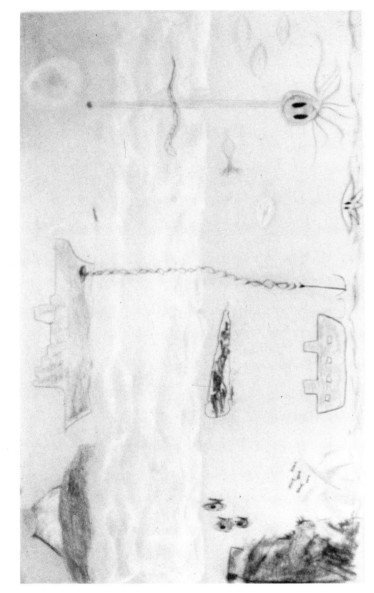

Sequence I. Group Formation. Stage 4: Unconscious. "UNDERWATER SCENE," August 25, 1966, Mural #4.

and withdrawal from the intimate relationships that the house symbolizes.

This is very likely the message of the group as each of its members contemplates his auto (self) trip through the hospital scene in search of the nutriments of emotional relationship.

In the following mural, a new and hysterically angry patient of Dr. Lukens', Mrs. Polanski, will participate. She is admitted in the throes of a desperate externalization of her feelings of inner deterioration. An insecure stranger to this country, she has developed brain damage, epilepsy, arthritis, and through impulsive overeating, has distorted her statuesque body structure. At times she refuses to leave Dr. Lukens' office and must be carried out bodily.

If the third mural structures the road to the unconscious, the fourth mural structures the arrival. "Underwater Scene" (#4), with its double layer, is typical of the mural of the unconscious which regularly portrays the interface between the source of all feeling and the world. The group attempts to control its inner aggressions by creating a scene of serenity.

This placid scene stands in opposition to the alternative choice expressed in the theme, "War." Aggressive outbreaks occur as an octopus warily points a periscope above the water, a volcano erupts in the distance, and finally, an attitude of general annoyance erupts into an argument. Mrs. Polanski complains that she is not allowed to express her feelings. There are allusions made to the power structure which exists above the water line. The ward's antiaggressive motif acts to suppress individual expressions of anger, thereby providing a nidus for the structure of the group as a loosely knit aggregate of beings, each keeping his separate place. Thus, the interaction between individual sources of aggression, and the external forces on the ward, produces the outline of a structure for the group.

Miss Serena draws the water line with an orange ocean liner perched on top. Beneath the water she draws a green eel which, she remarks, is able to escape from the octopus. Another contribution to this mural takes the form of a volcano which appears in the distance. These productions offer some confirmation of the belief that she fears she will be engulfed. The snake or the eel represents that aspect of her self which made it possible for her to escape from her subjugating aunt (the octopus). Her rage seeks an outlet in the volcano which continues the mountain motif. In this mural she is less able than the average group member to defend against her anger by imposing an attitude of serenity on herself. She had clearly come to this session to state her angry feelings. Wanting to know, "Does the mural have to have a topic decided upon by the group or can I just get up and draw anything that comes to mind." In other words, she wanted to know if she could vent the full range of her angry feelings without being restricted within the bounds of some placid scheme that would impose upon her the need to compromise or tone down her symbolic language. It is interesting that the suggestion by Mrs. Cooper to do an underwater scene comes just at this point—at the beginning—immediately following Miss Serena's question; and that Mrs. Polanski's follow-up suggestion was to depict the Vietnamese War. That Miss Serena's intense anger was shared by other members of the group became apparent by the immediacy with which it was picked up and conveyed in the following messages: Mrs. Cooper: "Let's keep it submerged," Mrs. Polanski: "Let's blast it into the open." Miss Serena's "I'm with you" in response to Miss Polanski's "War" theme suggestion is not at all surprising, coming as it does from one whose urge to let the battle rage is so overwhelming. Suggesting a moment later, however, that both themes might coexist indicates a sudden upsurge of conflict between maintenance of the defensive phase and submission to that side of her per-

sonality which demands greater outward expression of
her seething inner inferno. She finds an ally in Mrs. Polanski, who has similar conflicts concerning such expression. The rest of the group, Mr. Rappaport and Mrs.
Cooper, remain firm in their preference for the peaceful
"underwater scene." For them, safety is to be found in
the silent unconscious. Temporary resolutions of hostility
are the regular signal to move on to the next phase of
mural production, i.e., from theme selection to mural
drawing, or from drawing to discussion.

The peace versus war or serenity versus anger conflict
is played out all though the mural, Mrs. Cooper assuming the role of protagonist and meeting with strong but
silent resistance in Miss Serena. It is evident that Miss
Serena's verbal eruption during the discussion of the
mural had to do with feelings of being rejected by the
group when she had attempted to compete with Mrs.
Cooper as an influential member whose ideas were respected. It is interesting that Miss Serena's call to the
group to speak out through the media of the mural meets
with some resistance, yet she is encouraged to verbalize
her feelings as the session is about to end. This is an obvious reflection of the same ambivalence expressed by
Miss Serena during the theme selection stage of the
mural and which is also to be seen in her graphic contributions to the scene above and below the water line; the
eel, the ocean liner—the added water, the sun and finally
the erupting volcano, her last graphic statement.

Another interesting aspect of this group as it submerges to the unconscious is its sudden involvement with
color. More color has been introduced in this mural than
in any of those done previously. Miss Serena, who once
apologized for her exclusively excessive use of black,
now creates from her palette a green eel, an orange ocean
liner in blue outline, a yellow sun, a light blue and white
water line and a brown and red flaming volcano. Clearly,

Sequence I: Group Formation. Stage 5: Recombination. "ABSTRACT," September 1, 1966, Mural #5.

the increased use of color manifests an involvement with deeper levels of feeling.

During construction of "Abstract," (#5) anger is gradually confronted. The patients try to create new symbols and forms, anger toward one another is displaced to doctors and to the mural task itself. As the mural progresses, distorted broken-down forms are replaced by emerging meaningful shapes. There is particular evidence of anger toward Mr. Rappaport, who refuses to participate. The group begins to integrate its reaction to anger by collectively opposing those persons who embody that feeling. Miss Serena isolates her contribution to the mural by drawing with very heavy black lines. She reflects the group's attempt to improvise internal structure. This need is borne out of the lack of involvement—sensed by members of the group—on the part of the total staff which seems to be preoccupied with internal problems of its own in the realm of aggression. Their challenge to the Art Therapist, Mr. Blackman, to articulate to them the meaning and usefulness of the mural sessions was a call for more than just that. It was also a call for more overall staff involvement in their individual and collective problems. "What is this treatment supposed to do for us? Can you really help us? Do you really care? Can we really trust you? Will you give us controls?" These are some of the more basic issues implicit in their questions.

Miss Serena, who according to her own statement had suggested the abstract theme before the session began, continued to stand out as a catalyst for the group, as well as a reflector of its many dynamic facets. It is she who responds with her own immediate anger to the anger and indignation brought to the group by Mr. Rappaport, who announced, "I'm not going to do anything anyway," when the therapist asked that he be brought up to date after coming in late. Miss Serena countered his remark with, "I feel that you should. If I have to you should too. You're no better than me." This upheaval presages the rallying together of the patient group which is signalled by Mrs. Polanski's, "Let's do it." One should note that up to this point, and for the duration of the mural, Mrs. Cooper, who usually attempts to give direction, remains passively silent. There seems to be a realization on her part that her efforts at providing leadership had been totally submerged in the last mural session ("Underwater Scene," #4) and that there was now in process a movement for group constitution by which she or any other pretender to leadership could be destroyed. The group would now unify itself to prepare for its challenge to the staff, whose preoccupation with its own difficulties had begun to threaten the patients. What had been a search for individual trust was thus transformed into a struggle for total survival whereby the full strength of each participant (not just one) would have to be summoned. It is in the service of this end, the establishment of a collective unit, that the push for leadership on the part of both Mrs. Cooper and Mr. Rappaport are neutralized.

The group's attempt to integrate itself was, in part, an effort to relate as a whole to the staff. For the patients, being "in on" the doctor's discussion of the mural had more to do with seeing themselves as competent, equal and able to take care of themselves (if necessary) than it had to do with gaining a better understanding of the purpose and use of the mural. What the individual members of the group wanted least was a public interpretation of their very private symbols of communication. It is more likely that they were collectively asking for assurance that their individual productions were being used in each one's personal behalf. They were eager to understand the dynamics of their communications, and most of all, as Miss Serena seemed to express, they wanted to communicate on this level with their doctors. Miss Bernard's discussion with Mr. Blackman, the Art Therapist, about whether or not he was talking *at* the group or *with* the group might be seen as a need for reassurance as to the Art Therapist's confidential relationship to the group. In a sense, she is asking him the question, whose side are you really on, theirs (the staff's) or ours (the patients'). In mural #5 the aggression of the group begins to structuralize in terms of subject versus object, i.e., with us versus against us. This mechanism of splitting tends to segregate the patients as the "liberal" expressive faction, and the staff as the "conservative" suppressive faction.

"A Home" (#6) is a gentle welcome to a homesick new patient, Mr. Braverman, who is the first man to participate graphically. A stocky former patient of Dr. Isaacson, he has lost his verve, having become depressed over disappointments in his business. His own lack of assertion subjugates him to his business partner's will, and he feels as he broods, that his family is not on his side. He seeks, and finds, multiple assurances from the female patients that he is worthy of their understanding.

The mural scene is alive, as if the inhabitants are just out for the moment. As they create the mural, group members share their ideas easily. In accordance with its place in the creative sequence of expression, this mural structures a resolution of the original dilemma, i.e., how to form a group in the face of the danger of mutual hostility? Following the pattern of the staff's evolution, two opposing, but comfortable "camps" lending definition to each other take shape. A longing for fusion and reconciliation is created by the division. Thus, the mural poignantly expresses the wish to return home at the same time that a hospital-home split is made explicit. Inasmuch as a temporary resolution of aggressive conflicts has occurred, the expression of sexual themes can begin to surface. The increased energetic tone is also

Sequence I: Group Formation. Stage 6: Resolution. "A HOME," September 8, 1966, Mural #6.

characteristic of the economic gain of restructuring the group.

Miss Serena contributes an entire second home of her own, replete with tree, sky, swimming pool, birds and sidewalk. When members of the group comment on how comfortable her home looks, she answers that they can use her things. This represents the pleasant aspect of symbiosis, where each person can share the bodily comforts of the other. Miss Serena's penchant for symbiotic relationships facilitates the group's primitive differentiation.

The interchange of statements by the patients vis-à-vis their own and each others' symbolic contributions bears a quality of superficial sexual attraction. Mr. Braverman enjoys intensifying the rivalry he senses between Miss Serena and Mrs. Cooper. He tosses around compliments in much the manner of a spendthrift and the two women, each in turn, vie for the lion's share of his ingratiating attention and praise. Mr. Rappaport, on the other hand, is stiff, uncomfortable and distant, and his few verbal responses only serve to restate his determination to avoid active participation.

Mrs. Butler is a young married incipient schizophrenic who can not tolerate her own sense of self, with or without her husband. After Mrs. Polansky leaves, she does not attempt to compete directly with the two younger women. She does, however, attempt to prove that only she can interact supportively with Mr. Braverman as she helps him identify the colors after he tells the group that he is color blind. Perhaps she is hoping that he will eventually choose her as his close companion in this hospital "home."

The sexual by-play suggested in the pictorial symbols and the attendant dialogue emerging from this mural session is manifested by Mrs. Cooper at the very outset. She declares her sexual uncertainty toward Mr. Braverman from the very beginning. This is suggested in her empty, windowless house with the phallic chimney and her tentatively inviting door. At this point Mr. Braverman temporarily withdraws into a yearning for his own home, thereby avoiding the impulses brought on by these two seductive young women. In his dilemma, upon announcing, "Everyone's so good. I don't know what to do," he proceeds to draw windows which become the eyes of his tormented self, and then sketches a "downspout of water," the tear duct of his soul. He tells of his feeling of desolation at being separated from his family in the following words, "Only one thing is missing—people and kids." Immediately after, he begins to cry. Mrs. Butler adds yellow curtains, perhaps a handkerchief, to dry his tears. This is the nature of her responses to Mr. Braverman. It was she who answered his call for help in making his color selections. Mrs. Cooper's "doghouse" for Mr. Braverman's dog and Miss Serena's "I'd let you take a swim in my pool if you let me play golf," is further indication of the underlying contest between the two women to provide Mr. Braverman with the comforts of a home. Each wanted to communicate her singular identification with his pain. Each one wanted to mother him, hopefully in turn to be mothered and fathered by him.

The dialogue in most of the mural sessions involving Miss Serena is rich not only in sexual content, but in what is implied racially. Miss Serena, the only person of color in the group, announces, "I'm antisocial today. I'm not going to draw anything on *their* side." This remark is countered by Mr. Braverman's, "You're doing so well I wouldn't dare draw in your area." There are several such references throughout the session. Once the staff and the patients are split a reconciling tendency also becomes a force.

In this session Mr. Braverman, who is Dr. Isaacson's private patient, stands in for Dr. Isaacson. His presence facilitates the group's resolution of its early distrust by dividing the members up according to the difference in quality of feeling which he elicits in them. His coming signals Dr. Isaacson's return from vacation and his sudden participation in the milieu. The "welcome home" indicates a primary harmony between subject and object.

In "Metropolis" (#7), the resolution has been worked through and amplified. Hostility has been neutralized and overcome, and each person has his own section (or territory) in the mural as well as in the group seating arrangement, which is accorded some respect. The dissenter to the theme, Mrs. Polanski, wants to draw a rainstorm, but is easily overruled. The arching rainbow that dominates the scene connects the two "camps"—the rainstorm has been overcome. Group differentiation reveals itself in the following remarks:

"Each person has his own section."

"This is all mine."

"I don't mind if anyone draws in my Chinese section."

"Can I make a sun in your park?"

"Are we allowed in your park?"

No one will encroach on the territory of another without explicit permission to do so. In this respect, all group members will be alike.

In this session Miss Bernard is present, Mrs. Polansky is able to remain through the entire period and a new female patient joins the group. Mr. Braverman is the only man in the group, due to Mr. Rappaport's absence. Immersed in a sea of womanhood now, Mr. Braverman can no longer indulge in courtships like those of the previous session. He intuitively suggests that "each person have his own section in which to draw," a format which would permit each person to be separate. This suggestion was seemingly ignored or rather rejected by the rest of the

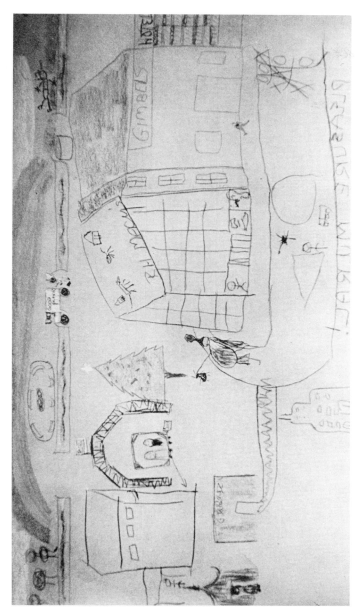

Sequence I: Group Formation. Stage 6, continued: Resolution. "METROPOLIS," September 15, 1966, Mural #7.

group. Later when Mr. Braverman attempts to move into Miss Serena's territory, "Green Gate Park," Mrs. Butler rushes to the "rescue" to make him a bed of soft grass to lie on before someone else, like Miss Serena, beats her to it. Mrs. Butler continues in her efforts to gain a symbiotic relationship with Mr. Braverman. He encourages her by consulting with her on the selection of colors. They sit side by side at one extreme end of the mural group opposite Miss Serena and Mrs. Cooper.

Mr. Braverman, the patients' present figure of strength, must allow equal access to himself by all those who seek him, a position which inevitably leads to his relative inaccessibility to all. Dr. Isaacson's present position is experienced in an analogous way by the staff.

Miss Serena, who is allowed to stake out a claim to the entire top 30 per cent of the mural board for her section of "Green Gate Park," asserts, "This is all mine." Later, she rather good-naturedly consents to have others enter her domain, but only with her permission and on her terms. She has reversed her original fear of being engulfed and now offers to take anyone into her own structure. Miss Serena has expansively carved out a pointedly separate but sharable identity for herself in the group. Her participation in the group's structural formation facilitates her own structural individuation.

In "Farm Scene" (#8) the nourishments, blandishments and multiple satisfactions have reached a peak and signs of disintegration begin to emerge. So many satisfactions are provided that they ultimately assume a surreal quality. During the mural session there is much teasing and camaraderie. A group spirit has evolved, yet there are signs that presage a new kind of hostility. The resolution of the initial problem is about to give way.

There is a noticeable shift in the seating arrangement for this mural session which finds the angry Mrs. Polansky holding fast to her central position. Miss Bernard and

Sequence I: Group Formation. Stage 6, continued: Resolution. "FARM SCENE," September 22, 1966, Mural. #8.

Mrs. Cooper, however, have moved completely over to the other end of the semicircle, near Mr. Braverman and Mrs. Butler and away from Miss Serena. Their former seats are now occupied by new patients. It is interesting to note that Mr. Braverman and Mrs. Butler have switched seats, which now places the former on the extreme end and the latter protectively between him and the two younger women, Miss Bernard and Mrs. Cooper. An overall view of this change in the seating arrangement reveals a more balanced distribution of old and new patients. Such a seating shift may constitute a defense against disintegration, an effort to maintain the group structurally by eliminating the physical division of old and new patients. The foci of potential hostility are spread in an even manner by this arrangement. Miss Serena's role in this session was overshadowed by Mrs. Cooper's dominant leadership. It is Mrs. Cooper who warns the group to submit to caution, not to overstep itself at this stage of its development. She accomplishes this by drawing a mouse and cheese in front of the "nasty cat after chickens" drawn by Mrs. Polansky. Mr. Blackman's suggestion that the cat has two choices is met with Mrs. Cooper's response, "He has no choice! He's done with if he doesn't take the mouse—you've heard of cat-eating chickens!" Stated another way, Mrs. Cooper is saying that the group has no choice but to play it cool and not bite off more than it can chew; that it's not yet a strong enough body to move for self-determination. Perhaps sensing the threat of disintegration of the group, Miss Serena, by contributing her family unit—the two school children, rooster, turkey and clothes line strung with pants and dress—is providing the strongest support for Mrs. Cooper's attempt to "hold the line." In calling for a more structured mural, the new male patient supports this position. The group begins to stretch the structure of its resolution as new problems are impending.

Sequence II: Group Differentiation (9/29/66–10/26/66)

Toward the end of September a new period is ushered in after the admission of several new active patients. Mrs. Polanski now feigns dramatic convulsions periodically; Mrs. Butler, increasingly inarticulate, regularly elopes from the ward; a third woman screams out her rage in sudden bursts of energy; Mr. Perlin, a self-indulgent, whimsical young schizophrenic man, adds further drama to the ward scene. His father, an esteemed scientist, was repeatedly forced to rescue his son from socially self-defeating escapades. Mr. Perlin seeks similar control on the ward. He will suddenly stop in his tracks, and in a flourish of physical and verbal gestures which belie immobility, cry out, "I'm paralyzed. I can't move. I can't talk. My body is going to pieces." He becomes Dr. Augress's first acute management problem. Mrs. Weil, an angry relative of a political figure, brings a sense of pressure to the ward. Her therapist, Dr. Lukens, is suddenly confronted with a whole new range of management problems—court orders have to be obtained; a powerful family must be conciliated; the staff requires direction in dealing with the patient's flagrant delusions. She is a pacing, preaching, painted caricature of the duchess in *Alice in Wonderland.* Now Dr. Lukens realizes the pressures that Dr. Isaacson has to contend with daily. Under the strain of sudden, often hostile, challenges the staff's personal roles must be defined and established in an atmosphere of increasing self-doubt and recrimination.

Mr. Blackman says of this period, "It was the beginning of everyone doing his own thing." The Ward Secretary says of this time, "The war between O.T. and Nursing began." Dr. Lukens states, "Each doctor wanted absolute authority to make decisions about his patients."

Nurses require definitive instructions when patients are disruptive. Doctors respond with uncertain and variable messages. Now the question of a liberal or a strict approach becomes an immediate and urgent decision. Precedents are sought. In mid-October, Dr. Lukens' patients (Mrs. Butler, Mrs. Weil and Mrs. Polanski) stage a series of "escapes." The one "resident" psychiatrist also "escapes," having decided to cut short his commitment to the ward.

In the aftermath of the escapes, Dr. Isaacson asserts greater authority on the ward. He is responding to outside pressure as concerned and influential families complain about the escapes. The liberal faction resents Dr. Isaacson's restrictions as he transmits the pressure to them. Disillusionment grows in the staff as omnipotent wishes are overturned. Dr. Isaacson's assertion, as well as Miss Conrad's insistence on the need for patient controls, reestablishes some stability by the end of October. Individual staff members become aware of the nature of their own functions and tend to restrict their own roles.

The emphasis on role definition is at its height at the time of the admission of Mrs. Weil. The fact that she must be admitted against her will and that her family has important political connections puts great strain on the staff when she escapes. The existing patient group is severely threatened by the disruptive quality of the new patients and by the care that they require.

Gradually, Miss Serena, Miss Bernard and Mrs. Cooper coalesce into a subgroup, which is initially held together by their shared feelings of hostility toward the new patients. Miss Bernard's actions and statements through October include the following:

a. She cuts herself with a mirror from a compact.

b. "Entertain us, after all we're not throwing tantrums or having seizures" (a reference to new patients).

c. Miss Bernard and Mrs. Cooper refuse to get out of bed: "Let's see what the nurse is going to do."

This type of taunting and needling grows as she and

her friends belittle the structure of the ward and make jokes about their therapists.

During this period Miss Serena[1] vacillates between a symbiotic and a separation-individuation type of relationship with her therapist, Dr. Lukens. It is punctuated by angry outbursts and ambivalence. She is one of the patients who threatens to escape from the ward when it is fashionable to do so. In therapy, she speaks of having run away from her aunt in the hills of Puerto Rico when she was a youngster and her fear of punishment upon return. She believes that her hostile "escapes" actually killed her aunt.

As they realistically portray the ward's structure, the group's fear of disintegration due to an influx of new patients is revealed. For the first time, sharing of rooms on the ward becomes a necessity rather than a choice. This is by far the largest mural group. The original patients are struggling to prevent incursion on their living space, while the newcomers are trying to carve out their own territory. As with the very first mural, "Floor Plan of a House" (#9) is pragmatic and essentially realistic. It is an actual portrayal of the ward. The limits of the ward are clearly defined in the mural as an attempt is made to preserve all structure.

In support of the interpretation that the older patients are struggling to maintain their territorial imperative, we hear Mrs. Cooper suggesting at the very beginning of this session that the group do an old West scene—"Pioneers in a circle—Cowboys and Indians—Let's close the door." Further emphasizing the fear of intruders, Miss Bernard adds, "A fort under attack." The cry for help goes out as rescue images such as "Rin-tin-tin" and "Lassie" are summoned. This is followed by the suggestion of themes

[1] The authors will now focus on Miss Serena and a few other key patients, in view of the large increase in the group's size during the following sequence of murals.

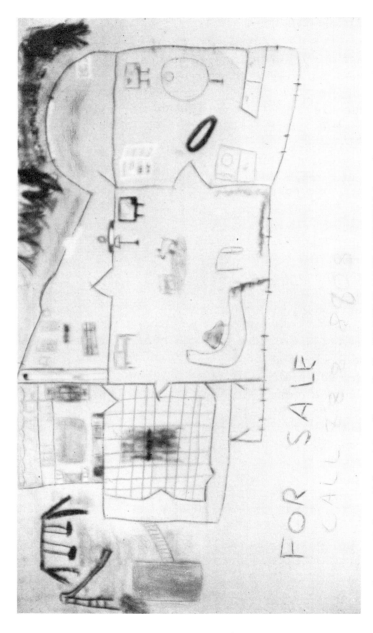

Sequence II: Group Differentiation. Stage 1: Reality. "FLOOR PLAN OF A HOUSE," September 29, 1966, Mural #9.

which echo the patients' yearning for more distant living space—"cactus, oasis, desert life." As if frightened by the image of the isolation that so much space implies, a new patient, Mrs. Goodhart, hastens to add, "People get lost in deserts." Mrs. Cooper, commenting on the increased group size says, "We need a theme with a lot in it." This statement may be interpreted as an expression of the need for a lot more in the ward scene to accommodate this growing community. When Mrs. Goodhart finally offers a much needed structure by suggesting a house sectioned off into rooms, the group is elated, shouting, "We did it!" From that point on the members proceed to redesign, refurnish and resupply their "one-family house," their 12-N, in an effort to make it meet their individual and collective needs. There is often an element in the initial presentation of reality which prefigures the group's resolution. In this case it is walling off larger or smaller compartments as the "murals" of the group's "mind."

In the mural drawing, Miss Serena makes a very commodious room at the upper left for herself. This is replete with a couch, stereo, bookcases, rug, and even a bar. She includes a room divider in her room. This contribution elicits envy in the other group members. Unlike the "metropolis" (#7) mural, she keeps this room exclusively for herself. She is defending her sense of separateness by using the mechanism of withdrawal and narcissistic investment which she had used at the very beginning of her stay on 12-N. Emphasizing this mechanism, her preferred seat during the mural sessions is at the end of the row.

The group is lively at the beginning of the next session. The search for a theme had begun when Mrs. Weil entered the room. Miss Bernard explains the mural's purpose and methods of procedure to Mrs. Weil, using the word "circus" in a description of earlier

themes. The circus idea was the actual theme in the comparable stage of the first sequence. This word seems to
have a trigger effect on Mrs. Weil, who has been venti-
lating in her usual confused manner while Miss Bernard
attempts to communicate. She reacts to the word by
storming out of the room in a state of verbal profusion,
indicating her resentment at being, "part of a circus."
When members of the group are questioned as to
whether they think the therapist, Mr. Blackman, should
invite Mrs. Weil to rejoin them, they indicate their ambivalence. Some are in favor and some are not. Mrs. Weil's
return is somewhat reluctantly accepted, as the tone of
her reentry suggests more disruption to come. Disregard-
ing the group's and the therapist's efforts to integrate her
into the orderly proceedings, Mrs. Weil approaches the
mural panel and begins to draw, over the protests of the
others. Her aggressive sweeping manner, as well as her
volatile production ("forest fire," #10A) reflects her hostile feelings. Overcome by her destructive impulse, she
rips the mural panel from the stand. It was clear to the
therapist prior to this episode that Mrs. Weil was appeal-
ing for structure and control. This could be surmised
from her message on the mural—"Prevent forest fires.
We don't want trees when we are rich and live in cas-
tles"—written just before she ripped down the panel. Mr.
Blackman asks Mrs. Weil to leave the room until she can
control herself. It is obvious that she can neither bring
herself under control nor leave the room voluntarily. He
therefore escorts her from the room. Another panel is
obtained and the group is asked to proceed with the
mural session. It is evident that a great deal of anger and
resentment are felt by members of the group toward Mrs.
Weil for the kind of behavior which tends to characterize
their environment as "crazy." They find it difficult to
verbalize their feelings and instead submit to a brief epi-
demic of giggling. There are a few individual comments

Sequence II: Group Differentiation. Stage 2: Statement. "FOREST FIRE," October 5, 1966, Mural #10A.

such as, "It isn't funny, she's really sick." As the second mural begins, Mrs. Weil returns to the room voluntarily and is given permission to rejoin the group on the condition that she try to exercise self-control and participate when it is her turn to do so. Having been assured by Mr. Blackman that order would be maintained and that she would be supported by him and the group in her struggle to hold down her anger, she agrees to cooperate. Mrs. Weil is accepted, albeit conditionally, back into the group membership. As the group tries to reorganize around its task, a "planet" mural is executed with Mrs. Weil's active and even articulate cooperation. Mr. Blackman's reassertion of control subsequent to Mrs. Weil's angry exit parallels Dr. Isaacson's role on the ward scene.

"A Way-out Planet" (#10B) wins over a jungle theme, but the jungle is very much in evidence as the animals hide. A peaceful enclave is partitioned off, only to be threatened by a meteor. The mechanism of separating off a single peaceful portion will later be elaborated into the resolution. Active disintegration of the group is portrayed. Defenses against aggression, emphasizing movement and flight, are rampant in the picture. This mural has the structural function of moving away from a presentation of the ward's reality toward a disguised version of the affective response. Animal forms conveniently represent the fear of destructive hostility.

Miss Serena draws a man-eating plant and a flying saucer. This reveals her oral aggression in the face of a threat to her own integrity, as well as her penchant for flight.

During this stage the reality problem is perceived, introjected and symbolized as a prelude to further defensive adaptations. These dynamics become necessary because the structure of the group is no longer adequate to deal with the forces in reality, or to deter the breaking through of violent acts and hostile feelings.

Sequence II: Group Differentiation. Stage 2: Statement. "A WAY-OUT PLANET," October 5, 1966, Mural #10B.

"A Country Place" (#11) defensively avoids open violence. Structurally, the mural is divided into one
well-organized, protected area and another which is
poorly differentiated. An airplane is depicted crashing
into the latter area. Then, one patient adds to another's
drawing, despite objections. This action violates the resolution of the first sequence. The cooperation by longer-
stay patients to produce a sheltered area of the mural
further prefigures the resolution. The functional significance of this mural in the sequence is the defensive
avoidance of open hostility. Neither violence nor the recognition of anger which signals violence can be tolerated.

Despite the fact that there are several suggestions, this
large group of 14 participants moves reluctantly toward
its decision upon a theme. When the group is asked by
Mr. Blackman why it is having such a difficult time making a decision, Mrs. Cooper refers to the fact that there
are so many more people in the group. Mrs. Cooper, a
long-time member of the group, has functioned quite
consistently as its arbitrator. Her contributions of cider
and apples provide food and drink for the inhabitants of
this pastoral scene. Her few verbal comments include a
call for agreement on the subject of requiring permission
to add to the work of another. She also emphasizes the
need for mutual respect among group members. She
seems to sense that things are about to get out of hand
and with the aid of Miss Bernard, succeeds in preventing
the group members from devouring one another. Even
Mrs. Weil, who found it so difficult to manage control in
the previous mural session, now rushes with a parachute
to rescue the group from Mr. Perlin's burning plane.
Miss Serena, perched on the extreme end of the semicircle, is prepared to take flight as she draws a number of
black birds and a sky. Another patient says, not so hu-
morously, "The birds is coming." This is a reference to
the Alfred Hitchcock movie in which countless numbers

Sequence II: Group Differentiation. Stage 3: Defense. "A COUNTRY PLACE," October 12, 1966, Mural #11.

of birds overwhelm and devour the members of a community. Once more her contribution reflects the group's dynamic orientation as she reveals the fear that her identity will be overwhelmed by the voracious environment. The imagery of oral sadism reflects the group's attempt to deal with the proposition that there is not enough for everyone.

"Land and Water" (#12) portrays the group as it submerges to the realm of its own respective unconscious territory in order to find a solution to its common problem. Members repeatedly voice respect for one another's property and artistic contributions. This mural, comparable to the "Underwater Scene" (#4) of the first sequence, employs a more refined effort at solution to the hostility than the mere evocation of serenity. There is greater emphasis on the privilege of individual or small group contribution. In the first sequence this stage was entirely underwater. Now the long-time patients, especially Miss Serena, Miss Bernard and Mrs. Cooper, can return to the comfort of their original détente with one another. They all agree that the land-water division is the best theme even though Mrs. Weil strenuously objects to any emotional undercurrents. The trio produces images of incorporation, octopus, fish-eating fish, as they bind their oral hostilities in order to reemerge with their unity intact.

Miss Serena begins by drawing a division between land and water, cutting the scene in half. This statement, which sets the tone for the actual drawing reveals again the way in which Miss Serena erects boundaries and territories to facilitate her movement through, around and away from the various danger areas depicted by the group in these mural sessions. There is a kind of covert agreement shared by Miss Serena, Miss Bernard and Mrs. Cooper to influence if not control the mural sessions. Mrs. Cooper is the more obvious leader, often

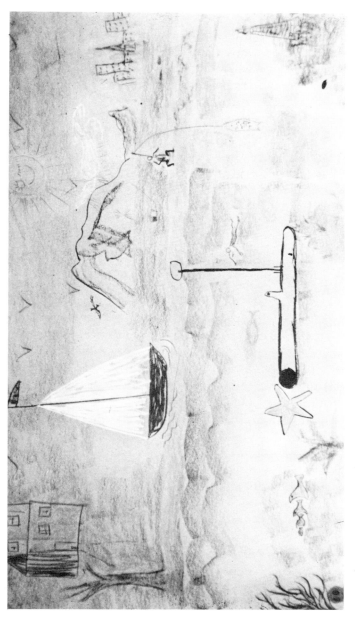

Sequence II: Group Differentiation. Stage 4: Unconscious. "LAND AND WATER," October 19, 1966, Mural #12.

prodding the group to begin the theme-selection discussion and vote on the drawing itself. Miss Bernard has become a more active partner in the assumption of this role, sharing a co-leadership with Mrs. Cooper. Miss Serena, the third member of the triumvirate, is not as verbally directive as the other two. She does, however, frequently set up the graphic spatial limitations within which or around which the rest of the group must work. Through her control of boundaries, Miss Serena not only attempts to harness her own hostility and limit her own self-concept, but she provides a general boundary for the group as well, thereby influencing the degree to which intimacy or isolation will prevail. She is accepted in this role. In this land and water mural, all but one of the 12 patients participate in the actual drawing. They are prolific in their contributions and profuse in their verbalizations. During the discussion period, the following exchanges occur.

New arrival (female): "I wish Mr. Perlin were here. I wish I could say it to him. He continually draws about destruction."

Mrs. Goodhart: "Well, I don't see it that way. His submarine is submerged but the periscope is sticking up. He's beginning to see." (Beginning to see he must limit his aggression to be a member of the chosen ones.)

Mrs. Foster: "I think so too."

Mrs. Weil leaves.

New arrival (male): remarks that Mrs. Weil's mountain was inappropriately drawn over a corn field.

Mr. Blackman remarks that the contributions under discussion are those of absent patients. (Mr. Perlin had been called out by his doctor. He did not "escape." Absent members are seen as extruded and as Mr. Perlin is being accepted into the group, his hostility is seen as being bound or incorporated by the group—affirming this connotation, the dialogue continues.)

Sequence II: Group Differentiation. Stages 5 and 6: Recombination and Resolution. "MUSEUM," October 26, 1966, Mural #13.

New arrival (female): (Re Miss Bernard's fish) "Big fish eating up little fish. That's very much like life."

Miss Bernard asserts it's only cute.

Miss Foster: "It looks like a family of four." (She wishes to join the triumvirate as will be seen in the next mural.)

New arrival (male) affirms that fish do eat each other in life.

The triumvirate talk among themselves.

Several patients make comments that infer they would like to break through their feeling of isolation and hostility.

New arrival (female): (to Miss Bernard) "By your two different pictures of fish, you see life in two ways. Both destructive and swimming together." (This remark confirms the group's current situation of overcoming hostility by forming a subgroup that cooperates to bind its anger.) In this mural of the unconscious, a subgroup actively incorporates new members into its own unity as a way of binding its oral aggression in the creation of a new structure for the group. This keeps the subgroup from being devoured. Other group members submit in order to control their own aggression, or they flee the threatening structure.

"Museum" (#13) depicts a resolution. It is dominated by three pumpkin faces in portrait form, each of which is a caricature of the patient who drew it. Individual facial characteristics are well demarcated. Miss Serena, Miss Bernard and Mrs. Cooper, who constitute the subgroup, are still favorites. During the mural drawing, the group process encourages formation of the subgroup's identity and utilizes its solidarity to withstand the pressures of hostility within the group.

Miss Serena begins by drawing an empty, black square. The next two contributors are Mrs. Cooper and

Miss Bernard, each of whom makes an adjacent, and slightly larger, black square. Mr. Perlin adds a black square with some content, and signs his name. The remaining patients cluster their drawings around the original, usually as variations; they draw picture frames of different colors or shapes. Then, Miss Serena adds a face to a square which is gilded and scalloped. The group responds, "Lovely." Mrs. Cooper adds a similar frame. A patient says, "You are copying Miss Serena." "You are right," she answers. Mrs. Goodhart says, "This shows the group interaction, but there is a fine difference. People really can't copy each other completely." Miss Bernard adds her face, whereupon other patients make joking references about doing the same thing.

The subgroup then quietly discusses its next move. A new male patient says, "I think there is a conspiracy here." Mrs. Cooper gets up out of turn, stimulated by this comment, and draws a pumpkin shape with an appended red ribbon. Miss Serena and Miss Bernard get up immediately and design the same kind of pumpkin. Mrs. Goodhart points out once again, "It doesn't matter about copying, each one is still slightly different. You're each individuals." In response to this, the elite three argue momentarily about whether stems are green or brown. Then Mr. Perlin blocks out his signature, claiming that he feels funny being the only one who signed.

Miss Serena adds a green as distinct from a brown stem to the pumpkin. Her portrait has a luscious red mouth and enticing eyes. She emphasizes sexiness and those external adornments which accord with her own appearance. By strengthening her own external image, she reinforces her individuality. Mrs. Cooper and Miss Bernard similarly add individualized features to their faces. In the end the group discusses the differences among the three faces: angry, seductive and happy. The group accepts the way in which the trio works together. At this point, the original reality problem of this sequence can be restated: How can group disintegration be avoided despite the influx of new patients? The answer, clearly portrayed, is that the oldest subgroup shows the way to individuated cooperation.

An examination of the entire sequence just completed indicates that oral incorporative imagery flourishes throughout. From the nourishing farm scene (#8), with its cat-eating chickens, the last mural in the first sequence, the imagery continues in Miss Serena's bar in the floor plan (#9) mural, to the multicolored fruit tree of the planet (#10B) mural, to the cider and apples of the country place (#11). Miss Serena's voracious birds of that mural mark a transition to imagery of being eaten rather than being fed. This is focal in the fish-eating fish of land and water (#12). In the resolution mural (#13) identity is expressed as edible pumpkin heads. Thus the hostile oral-aggressive drive derivatives are bound through the formation of a subgroup the members of which have incorporated one another's identities.

Sequence III: Group Empathy (11/3/66–12/8/66)

During the period of November through the first third of December, the staff group experiences a reality context in which Dr. Isaacson's attention is minimal whereas his authority is manifest. Dr. Isaacson issues three memos on one day in November. They are to "set things straight" for the unit. One is a statement of authority, another an extension of authority and rank, and the third, which is circumvented, contains admonitions about using first names with patients. Although superficially compliant, the staff displaces hostility to Dr. Augress. A sense of loss is engendered by the departure of two young nurses, and by the near simultaneous discharge of several pa-

Sequence III: Group Empathy. Stage 1: Reality "HEAVEN AND HELL" (no mural record), November 3, 1966, Mural #14.

tients. Dr. Isaacson, ineluctably, is concerned with the ward's financial condition.

Late in November, two nurses are hired who have worked at the same hospital as has the Head Nurse. They replace the nurses who have decided to return to Medical and Surgical nursing. Both of the new nurses are over 40 years of age. Miss Spodney believes in "a strongly structured environment that emphasizes the patient's health potential." The other, Mrs. Reilly, becomes notorious for her unorthodox, warm methods in working with patients. The stabilizing presence of these nurses during a period of some new admissions facilitates formation of a staff group that is more aware of its inner emotional necessities.

In early November the patients are beset by anger at the staff as they sense the staff's preoccupation and loss of interest. The patient group, as well as the staff, must cope with the loss of key members. Mrs. Cooper, a member of the subgroup triumvirate, is discharged at this time. The present sequence of murals reveals a great deal about a group's creative method of coping with object loss, through a mechanism of identification with the aggressor.

The authors do not have available the protocol for the mural of November 3rd. The title "Heaven and Hell" (#14) suggests that it is a reality-bound mural depicting the ward milieu. To lend substantiation, one notes that the initial mural of Sequence IV presents the ward scene as Hell, i.e., Herzl Inferno (#25). The title also implies object loss with attendant mental pain. The entire sequence contains a dawning anticipation of the future. The next stage of the sequence is signalled, once again, by an animal scene.

"Zoo" (#15) states the problem of angry withdrawal from one another on two accounts. First, some of the key patients are in preparation for their departure from the

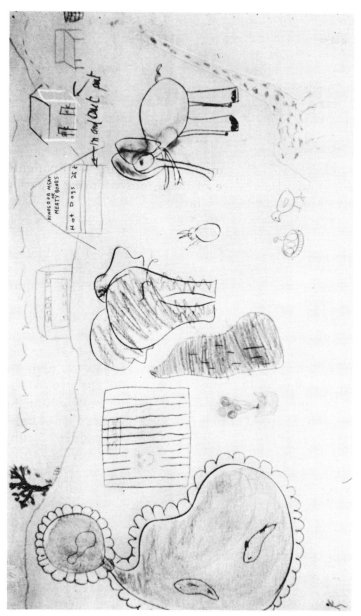

Sequence III: Group Empathy. Stage 2: Statement. "ZOO," November 10, 1966, Mural #15.

ward and, second, as the group remains together the question of increased intimacy becomes a problem. The animals are portrayed half inside and half outside the cages, semirealistically representing the flow of discharges and admissions.

During the mural session people constantly walk in and out. Some patients are missing. There are many anal references: the rear ends of animals, garbage cans, a toilet called "output." The tone suggests exasperation, each animal noticeable withdrawing from the others. The mural illustrates a scene of multiple lost objects. Later in the sequence the whole hospital ward becomes a lost object. In the discussion, Miss Bernard points out that there is only half a zoo. She feels the group's unhappiness over the loss of Mrs. Cooper. Withdrawal and depression are apparent.

Miss Serena draws a seal in a pool. When another patient follows this by drawing two seals in a pool, Miss Serena is angry. The anger alludes to a lack of bathroom facilities, especially the insufficient number of bathtubs to serve all the patients. Four of the rooms are equipped with tubs, while the rest have only showers. Frequently, Miss Serena would complain of feeling snubbed, or that people were purposely using words that she could not understand. In her desire to use another patient's bathtub, Miss Serena had the sympathy of the "have not" staff. Miss Serena also draws the sun as she tries to avoid an impending depression. The overdetermined images of anality indicate the group's retentive hostility as it is forced to part with an object perceived as part of the patient "body."

In "Geometric Forms" (#16) withdrawal is in full swing. The diminished group of six patients in attendance during this mural session were feeling ashamed and exposed to view. The escapist themes suggested include, "Circles, Geometric Forms, The Earth in 5000 B.C. or

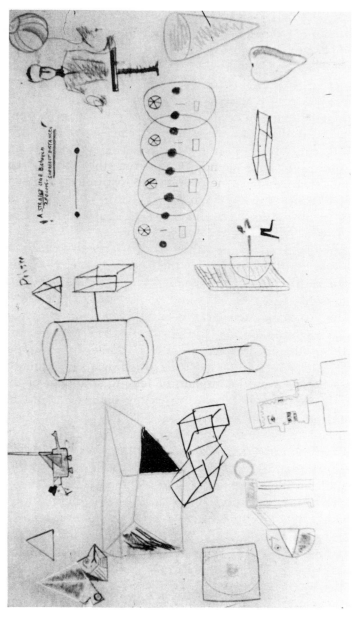

Sequence III: Group Empathy. Stage 3: Defense. "GEOMETRIC FORMS," November 17, 1966, Mural #16.

1,000,000 B.C., Fashions in the Future, and Real Estate on the Moon." These themes present movement away from reality toward the stage of unconscious confrontation with the problem of separation and loss. There is further evidence of the patients' sense of reticence and their desire to escape in such statements as Mrs. Goodhart's, "They're [the staff] going to have a hard time. They won't be able to tell anything from this mural. They won't be able to tell if it's in proportion or not." Mr. Perlin later states, "I would have been happier if all [the group] were here. There's no reason to do it if not everyone is doing it. I feel like my drawings are like those of a four-year-old. Yet, in other ways, I'm like a man. What will the doctor think?"

Miss Serena, on the other hand, states that she liked the fact that the group was small, pointing out that she is more comfortable in a smaller group. It was she who suggested circles but in spite of her insistence that she wished to draw circles, she began the mural by drawing a red triangle (anus?). It is important to note in connection with her stated preference for a smaller group, that she suggested subdividing the group further by offering to draw a line down the center of the mural panel so that one group could do geometric forms while the other could indulge in whatever it felt like doing. She is tempted to withdraw into narcissism once again rather than graphically depict those elements which symbolize her reality and express her most intense feelings. Her red triangle in the upper left corner of the panel tells at once of her triangular personal relationships, the nature of which often prompted her withdrawal to a position of angry isolation. Considering her two sisters and what occurred in that triangular relationship to precipitate Miss Serena's flirtation with suicide, highlights the nature of her involvement with Miss Bernard and Mrs. Cooper. Conceivably Mrs. Cooper's departure produces angry

Sequence III: Group Empathy. Stages 4 & 5: Unconscious and Recombination. "3000 A.D.," December 1, 1966, Mural #17.

withdrawal and a longing to search for a state of fusion once again, focussed on Miss Bernard and Dr. Lukens.

The use of geometric forms provided some members of the group with an avenue of escape from the anxiety-provoking material which would have given full expression to their feelings, while it was utilized by others to allow such material to emerge in less threatening form. To put it another way, some members of the group used this mode of expression as warriors would use their shields to cover their retreat, while others used the shields to protect their advance. There was to be sure a great deal of anger and resentment in the group which found only moderate expression through innocuous verbalizations and evasive graphic symbols. The mural presents such aspects of characterologic defense against anal derivatives as compliance and defiance.

The following week is Thanksgiving and there is no mural session. Dr. Isaacson responds to the mood of apathy and a drop in the census by proclaiming that the open-door policy is in jeopardy, and stating that more patients must be admitted. His response is as specific as a correct interpretation.

The patients assemble for the next session in a high-spirited manner, in contrast to their reluctant, depressed mode of entry over the past few sessions. Their exuberance was expressed in Mr. Perlin's exclamation, "I'm so excited, I can't wait!" which was accompanied by a lively skipping gesture toward the mural panel. In spite of their spirited entry and efforts to ward off unpleasant feelings, some degree of agitation and depression could be felt. Their uneasiness was apparent in the shifting of seats between Mrs. Weil and Miss Foster. The patients spoke of the "hospital" and various destructive events, questioning the ability of the milieu to protect them and help them in controlling their impulses. Several group members expressed selfish concern about their own individual problems and what the future held in store. In the drawing phase their symbols had very personal symbolic significance; yet gradually, concern and interest in a unified group expression emerged.

"3000 A.D." (#17) is a mural of unconscious confrontation with the problem of partial object loss. It is a world of the future in which the hospital itself becomes a living, breathing entity. It is replete with robot people, home-style IBM computers, and carnate dwelling places. A large sun bleeds into the hospital, further verifying the vivification that is occurring.

The double layering that is characteristic of the topographic shift to the unconscious is seen. Fish appear swimming in the water. The focus of the mural is Miss Bernard's living house, a personification of the institution. The aggressor has been lost and internalized by staff and patients alike. The patients have turned the hospital into an inner image. For the group a momentous psychological event has occurred in the form of a shared inner structure. The members replace in fantasy what they have lost in reality. The mural's imagery insists that all dead things can live in the brain.

Miss Serena's first contribution is the written statement, "Hospital of the Future," about which she indicates one will have different views depending upon one's state of sickness or health. This statement reflects her identification with the therapist who has been stressing the importance of distancing herself from her psychopathology in order to view it as an objective phenomenon. He has asked her to see the frightened little girl who clings to her aunt one minute and wants to kill her the next. Miss Serena draws two animals, a larger one and a smaller one. Another patient comments that they are devouring each other. Then Miss Bernard, who rooms with Miss Serena, says that the animals are mother and daughter. Another patient corroborates that this is her impression also. Then Miss Serena draws in the implements of suicide: a rope, knife, and drugs. The conjecture during the last mural that Miss Bernard would become a focus of symbiotic feelings for Miss Serena finds verification here. Certainly Miss Serena is turning her aggression onto the internalized object representing simultaneously, Miss Bernard, her sister, her aunt, and the therapist. In order to preserve the object in its infantile symbiotic setting, she feels impelled to leave the hospital and terminate her therapy. Having admitted the object into her inner world she is vulnerable to a reflux of aggression from it onto her infantile self.

In the postmural discussion, Miss Serena's animals are viewed repeatedly by the other group members as mother and daughter figures devouring one another. Through a common sense of loss, the group members have developed a shared imagery which enables them to appreciate the inner imagery of a given member. The hospital itself becomes vital as it is incorporated by individual selves.

Thus the group follows Dr. Isaacson's edict to shut the door and increase patient population. The group members survive the passive loss of part of themselves by actively and aggressively bringing in the person or institution responsible for their loss, and by identifying their own external structure with that of the aggressor. In this way they can identify with the whole incorporated object although there is still the danger that the individual's own self can be lost in the process. Introducing a new object so deeply into the ego brings new peril to the autonomy of the self.

In "Sightseeing in Metropolis" (#18), another mural of resolution, new structures are employed to provide the solution to the suicidal theme that was introduced the

Sequence III: Group Empathy. Stage 6: Resolution. "SIGHTSEEING IN METROPOLIS," December 8, 1966, Mural #18.

prior week. Crosscurrents are present as a number of new patients attempt to introduce a circus or jungle theme in order to work out their entrance into the group. However, the more senior patients prevail as they seek to resolve their own sense of loss before relating to the new conditions of the ward.

The patients help to control the suicidal impulses in one another. They also strive to keep all group members within the group. The person who draws the Towers Building offers to let others put windows in it. A missile is directed against it, but another patient puts up interceptor planes. This new attention to one another's inner life is seen again when a patient portrays herself on a bridge railing.

Miss Serena comments wryly that she wants people to know that she did not draw it. After her comment, another patient sketches in a guard rail to the bridge. This interplay illustrates Miss Serena's trust in the group's ability to help control her own self-destructive impulses. Miss Serena proceeds to draw a series of rather lifeless stick figures: first a man and a woman, followed by a whole family group. She is seeking self-protection within the group structure. In her therapy she reveals her fear of being alone on the street. At the same time she describes the feeling of being a little girl in a world of adults.

In the end of this mural the patients portray themselves on a public plaza, with the comment, "Let there be peace." As patients strive to protect one another from inward-directed aggressions as well as outward, a feeling of group understanding is created. In this sequence partial object loss is overcome through identification with the controlling, and adult, object. The group identifies, each with the controlling aggression of the leader, forming external ties from its common bond, which are stronger than any individual impulses of fight or flight.

Sequence IV: Group Power (12/15/66–1/26/67)

The big cry in December is, "Fill up to capacity." Ten patients are admitted in one month. Four are very influential in creating problems and growth for the unit. Miss Siegel is a young schizophrenic woman—a small, but explosive dynamo. Her penetrating wit is usually expended on her imaginary companions, but when it is directed outwardly, the ward quakes. Mrs. Woodward is a wealthy alcoholic sophisticate who does not appreciate the naiveté of the young nurses. The passing of her years is a source of great narcissistic injury, and a factor in her alcoholism. Young Miss Meyers becomes a favorite of Miss Marsh. She is a gentle, plump, vulnerable schizophrenic girl who is prone to sudden, dramatic, physically abusive regression.

The majority of the nurses favor Miss Marsh's easy, nondisciplinarian, kindly methods. But some nurses spend hours commiserating with favorite patients, while neglecting others. As Miss Conrad attempts to impose strictures on some of the questionable judgments, the nurses openly rebel. Much of this rebellion is heightened by Mr. Gordon's countertransference conferences with nursing. As this conference stimulates the expression of anger and feelings of rebellion, the nurses turn to Dr. Isaacson to restore order. Mr. Gordon's workshop is dissolved as the open expression of dissension becomes intolerable to Miss Conrad and to Dr. Isaacson.

The fourth influential patient is Mr. Novick, a young, Catholic, part-time artist who is addicted to a common tranquilizer. He is admitted for withdrawal from the drug and is assigned to Dr. Augress. The drug is frequently found in the patient's possession during the year he is hospitalized. There are numerous discussions about his care and it is debatable whether he can receive the type of therapy on 12-N that he needs. He begins his stay by

whining and crying, blaming the doctors who had origi-
nally provided him with access to the drug and the
competitiveness of the artistic world. His infantilisms elic-
it mothering from several nurses. After a period of some
weeks, he becomes "manly," informing patients and
staff that he is a judo expert. He also begins seducing
female patients, enters flirtations with two or three of the
nurses, and develops a coterie of male followers, especially his room-mate, Mr. Perlin. His predominance extends into the mural sessions, which he attends regularly
for the first six months of his stay. The first known
overtly sexual behavior on the unit is that between Mr.
Novick and Miss Meyers.

Mr. Novick's status as one who can sexually tease or
socially intermingle with the staff is one example of loos-
ening barriers between some staff and some patients.
Another example occurs at a Christmas party given in
Miss Serena's room on Christmas eve. Certain staff
members attend accompanied by guests. It is at this party
that Miss Serena meets her future husband, Mrs. Rohmer's son. She carries on a secret courtship with him for
several months. The spirit of Dr. Isaacson's warning
against using first names is thus circumvented.

During December and January the staff works hard
under Dr. Schwartz' increasingly liberal direction to meet
the challenges of patient care. The unit doors are re-
opened and the staff feels that he will respond to their
grievances. Gradually, Dr. Schwartz begins to draw fire
himself, centered at first on the belief that he expects his
own patients to receive special consideration.

The sudden flooding of new patients threatens to overthrow the solutions which have been worked out by the
patient group. The older, elite patient group insists that
its place in the dining room is being usurped. There are
displays of insensitivity, selfishness and competition
among the predominately female patient population. Com-

Sequence IV: GROUP POWER. Stage 2: Statement. "JUNGLE," December 15, 1966, Mural #19.

petitive feelings also disrupt the staff's mood of mutual understanding. Phallic aims of domination and possessive intimacy are expressed.

The grouping of patients at the Public Plaza in the last mural (#18) of the sequence probably represents the reality stage of the new sequence, as the patients are crowded together in a cooperative body. Now they are watchful and waiting, ready to withstand attack, allied against the invading hordes of new "animals." In "Jungle" (#19) aggression is neutralized at every turn. Group protection wins out over group aggression. Older members repel all attacks from newer members. The patients interact freely both at a verbal level, and by adding to one another's drawings. A consolidation of the last resolution of mutual protection is apparent.

At the beginning of this session there is an attempt on the part of two of the new group members to deny the aggression about to be displayed. One starts by suggesting a "peaceful scene in the country." This is followed by Mrs. Woodward's communal, "Kibbutz" The next suggestion is offered by Miss Foster, one of the group members with seniority, who is the first to introduce an aggressive theme, "Hunting Scene or Jungle." Miss Foster, who is preparing to return to her work as a social worker for the handicapped, partially fills the role of mural arbitrator vacated by Mrs. Cooper. A vocal, recently admitted, adolescent boy thinks that a "Bar Room" or "Harem" would be "groovy" themes until Miss Foster's "Jungle" moves him to question the need for a theme at all. But by this time the vote is already taken by Miss Foster, who is for this session the unchallenged leader of the group.

Miss Serena draws a striped giraffe portraying herself as the aloof observer who needs to see through, over and beyond the thicket and be equipped to move out of harm's way in time, at least with the fleetness of a zebra. Sensing through her own hostility the impending danger to Miss Serena's "giraffe," Mrs. Woodward provides it with background foliage which the adolescent boy calls "camouflage." After this Miss Bernard draws a lion to attack Miss Serena's giraffe. This is objected to by Miss Foster and Mrs. Woodward, who ask, respectively, "Why attack the giraffe?" "Why so hostile?" Miss Foster moves ambivalently to protect the giraffe by drawing a hunter. Miss Bernard, understanding the message, asks, "Is he aiming at my lion?" Later on Miss Serena provides added protection for her "giraffe" by drawing "Tarzan," guardian of the jungle's gentler animals, with muscles flexed. Miss Foster, not trusting Miss Bernard's striped "friendly jungle snake," strengthens Miss Serena's "giraffe." That the jungle has its violent as well as its peaceful nature is no doubt known to Miss Foster. Hence one might ask why she felt moved to suggest this particular theme. She apparently senses the mood of the group, which is a reflection of her own mood. She can, therefore, anticipate the imminent aggression and attempt to assume the role of protector, to save the group from internecine warfare, thereby earning its gratitude and its approval of her leadership. Why does Miss Bernard play into this by symbolically attacking Miss Serena, her triumvirate buddy, through the latter's own "giraffe" symbol? Of course it's a ruse. By leading the campaign of aggression she avoids being attacked by it. By using Miss Serena as a decoy, she redirects the aggression so that it is used to defend rather than to attack. It is Miss Bernard who places first a tree, then an ICBM and an antimissile missile beneath a plane which is threatening to drop its bombs on the jungle. Miss Serena's "peaceful family" suggests an appeal to the group to conciliate and get itself together. In this mural the group states the danger of shifting foci of group power. Miss Bernard and Miss Foster attempt to preempt the aggressive expression, presaging Mr. Novick's coup. The image of a strong male protector is introduced by the group.

On December 22 a decisive phenomenon occurs. Just as the discussion of a new theme is set, a (relatively) new patient, Mr. Novick, strides into the mural room and suggests a "Cape Cod" (#20) theme. The group immediately accepts his suggestion. He draws the entire mural while the group makes minor peripheral contributions. This manner of choosing the theme and conducting the session has many striking ramifications. First, it accords with the defensive phase of the sequence in which the group flees from its problem. The problem of this sequence is how to deal with jealous aggression in the absence of a given leader. Mr. Novick quickly assumes the role of patient protector. The suddenness suggests that his power originates in another source. Presumably, after the identification of the group with Dr. Isaacson as an authority figure, he has been projected to be embodied by Mr. Novick. A parallel phenomenon occurs in the investiture of Dr. Schwartz. Mr. Novick represents the power strivings of new patients, while suggesting the promise of omnipotence for those with seniority. His mural, since he is an artist, is a showpiece of which all can be proud. It portrays a scene of utter tranquility and peace, with formal artistic balance, sweep and scope.

Mr. Novick puts to good advantage his apparent virility and the mental agility of an addict, attributes which place him in a position of dominance on the ward. The patients avoid feeling depressed and alienated at Christmas season by identifying with his strength. Eventually, his stay on the ward becomes a contentious dilemma for the staff. The rebellious nurses want to protect him and treat him despite his disruptive behavior. Dr. Schwartz doubts his sincerity and is unsure about keeping him on

Sequence IV: Group Power. Stage 3: Defense. "CAPE COD," December 22, 1966, Mural #20.

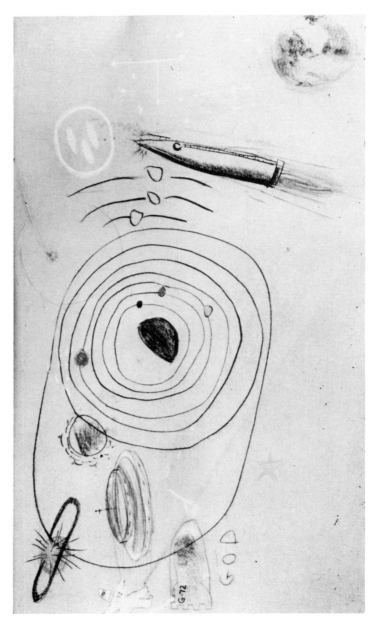

Sequence IV: Group Power. Stage 3: Defense, continued. "OUTER SPACE," January 5, 1967, Mural #21.

the ward. A decision to discharge Mr. Novick would put Dr. Schwartz in closer alliance with Miss Conrad. But Dr. Isaacson's future role in the ward's politic is an enigma.

Miss Serena adds a shore next to the lighthouse drawn by Mr. Novick. Her contribution is relatively more independent than that of the other group members. She finds a protector in the man whom she meets at the Christmas party and declares her independence from the group.[2]

In the mural of January 12, 1967, Mr. Novick continues to consolidate his power, until it reaches tyrannical proportions. He draws a "Country Scene" (#22) uninhabited by people, comprising a unity centered about a single house. One patient attempts to repel the new leader, but he is frightened and retreats. At the moment of Mr. Novick's power consolidation, Miss Serena and Miss Bernard exit from the group, on the pretext that they are needed for babysitting. Actually, they go to visit Mrs. Cooper, the third member of the old triumvirate. Miss Serena makes no contribution to the mural and, significantly, it is her last attendance at this group function. Mrs. Cooper has returned to her husband. She and Miss Bernard are increasingly involved in therapeutic relationships with Dr. Evans.

The next mural, "Fishing Village" (#23), continues the motif but at the same time reveals movement in the direction of the unconscious. Patients begin to assert their right not to have their contributions altered by Mr. Novick. The price of order has become too high and a rebellion is stirring.

At the beginning of this session there seems to be a need for a total gathering of strength within the group, as a moment is taken to account for each of the missing members. Having decided that enough of the member-

---

[2] The protocol for January 5, 1967 is missing. Mr. Novick does not attend. The "outer space" (#21) theme continues the defensive movement away from the ward's reality.

Sequence IV: Group Power. Stage 3: Defense, continued. "COUNTRY SCENE," January 12, 1967, Mural #22.

ship is present and that they need not wait for the arrival of Mr. Novick, they begin to do a little muscle flexing as is evidenced by their energetic push for a theme, independent of Mr. Novick's leadership. Theme suggestions range from a peaceful "Lake Placid," a bizarre exploration of the "Inside of the Brain," to "Vietnam" and a "Bar Room Scene." These themes each reflect the group's movement to an unconscious place of rebellion. The "bar," though not the selected theme, is nevertheless included in the mural. It offers an intoxicating release of rebellious impulses. In a hospital setting the patients and staff often call for controlling medication when anxiety levels reach a high point. Seen in the context of the mural as it relates to the inner needs of the patient group, the "Bar Room Scene" suggestion implies the existence of the bartender/doctor or barmaid/nurse, all with their measured shot-glasses of medicinal potions. Medication, or drugs, can offer the illusory sense of potent self-sufficiency which Mr. Novick embodies.

It is significant that Mr. Novick's entrance elicits a spontaneous response on the part of several group members who rush en masse to the panel. The effect is that of a phalanx in defense of the group's right to self-assertion.

Mr. Novick, through the use of his superior graphic skill, is a formidable problem for the group. The question is how to harness his powerful gift of expression to serve rather than manipulate and dominate the group.

During this confrontation Mr. Novick attemps to recoup his losses by becoming the group's drawing instructor. In his most grandiose manner he reminds his fellow patients of the lessons he has had in perspective as he proceeds to redraw and enlarge upon their contributions. During this demonstration two of the patients leave the room. Mrs. Hecht is the first to voice objection to Mr. Novick's dominant maneuvers, insisting that he not change any aspect of her drawing of water and rocks. She also objects when he structures the outlines of trees to which a very timid Mrs. Woodward adds color. Her resistance is strengthened by the act of drawing her own trees with which she expresses great satisfaction. While this very dynamic interplay between Mr. Novick and Mrs. Hecht intensifies, the rest of the group, encouraged by her defiant stand, provides her with a continuous flow of graphic support. One by one and two by two they go up to the mural and add their contributions. Their increased participation is in spite of rather than because of Mr. Novick's suggestion that more people get up and draw. His actions, which speak more loudly than his words, would have succeeded in totally squelching a group less committed to rebellion.

During the struggle in this "Fishing Village" (#23) scene, Mrs. Hecht rushes to the panel to create the "sky" which, according to Mr. Novick, has been his intention. Then there is a stream of admonishment from the other patients as he begins to provide the finishing touches. The statements include:

Mrs. Hecht: "It [the Fishing Village] doesn't look very Italian; it looks more like Maine." (This "put-down" comment suggests Mr. Novick's inability to usurp and deflect the spirit of the original theme proposal.)
Male Patient: "If you kill my surf, I'll put it right back."
Mrs. Woodward: "Don't make it [the sky] so cloudy and grey."

Mr. Novick at the point of the latter statement is adding an "angry" red to Mrs. Hecht's blue sky. In response to Mrs. Woodward's instructions, he draws a partial view of the sun behind the clouds, symbolizing and foretelling his own eclipse. When Mr. Blackman asks the patients to cite similarities between this mural and the preceding one ("Country Scene," #22), Mr. Novick's reply that it

Sequence IV: Group Power. Stage 4: Unconscious. "FISHING VILLAGE," January 19, 1967, Mural #23.

"looks less tranquil and is beginning to have people" is an allusion to how he sees the group.

The work of the unconscious has been the massive shift of aggressive forces onto the image of a single person. A common channel of assertive aggression is created. This shift unifies the group as it allows individuals to relate on the basis of a common internal assumption. In addition to its autoplastic function, i.e., reactive domination of emerging drive impulses, the internalized representation of the aggressor can now be used as a vehicle for directing aggression in alloplastic, assertive ways. Mr. Novick can enact this function for the group, just as Dr. Schwartz can do so for the staff.

In the following mural, resolution occurs as the deposing of the tyrant is depicted. There is great difficulty in choosing the theme. The "tyrant" theme loses to "Carnival" (#24). The mural is divided by a black line into a background and a foreground. In the foreground the patients are gathered, partly in an animal guise, looking for thrills and action on a roller coaster and a ferris wheel. In the background a tightrope figure threads his way warily. "I hope he falls," says Mr. Perlin, who is Mr. Novick's ambivalent crony. The figure on the parachute jump is hanging in a strange position. The implication that Mr. Novick is being deposed amid a spirit of celebration and revolution is clearly present in the dialogue of the protocol. The "Carnival" background in which the fantasied tragedy is to take place represents another of the patients' many versions of 12-N. In this one, the ward not yet clearly defined, is implemented with the objects of dangerous excitement and pleasure. There is an element of precarious thrill in carrying out their coup. They are caught up in a roller coaster ride from whose steep turns and sudden drops there is no turning back. The merry-go-round and ferris wheel suggest the group's sensitivity to its involvement in a process which once begun

Sequence IV: Group Power. Stages 5 & 6: Recombination and Resolution. "CARNIVAL," January 26, 1967, Mural #24.

must come full cycle to its logical sequential conclusion. Mr. Novick's parachute jump is a preparation for taking his own way out.

The game booths added by Mrs. Woodward are for those less daring, who nevertheless desire to share in some of the thrills of chance. For those who would rather indulge themselves with even less risky pleasures, a food-vending cart is provided by Mrs. Weil. For those who would just like to sit this one out or have a place to rest after the dizzying merry-go-round, a park bench is added by petulant Mrs. Hecht.

Mrs. Polansky's "net" beneath the tightrope walker expresses the group's remaining positive ambivalence toward Mr. Novick and its awakening guilt at the prospects of usurping his role. To summon renewed strength in the "walker," she adds an acrobat which balances on the stick he carries. No doubt the added burden will serve to increase the inevitability of his fall. Eventually the group must pay the price for its part in his demise, perhaps at Mr. Rabins' "Carnival" ticket booth. The following month's sequence elaborates on this point. The spirit of revolution and rebellion is present in the staff members as well. They move to begin group discussions and to liberalize the ward. The spirit of celebration reveals, once again, the excess of energy which becomes available after a structural reorganization. In this case aggression is no longer used exclusively for defensive purposes, but may be implemented and channeled through the image of a controllable leader. The staff and the patients have each tried to create a vulnerable scapegoat. However, neither Dr. Schwartz nor Mr. Novick proves to be without resources.

4

THE DEVELOPMENT
OF GROUP SCHIZOPHRENIA

Sequence V: Group Identification (2/2/67–3/23/67)

TEN MORE patients are admitted in January, one of whom is Mrs. Popidopolus, a middle-aged woman, who was the last of 11 children. Her immigrant parents had neither time nor enough food to give her when she arrived. She therefore suffered a great sense of neglect and abandonment. On the ward, to compensate for her position in her natural family, she tries to be a model of maturity in the group, always supporting group action, particularly when such action is taken to overthrow a powerful group member. In return, she constantly demands to be treated as the favored child. In February there are two more admissions. Five of the new patients are adolescents, one of whom is Miss Allen. Another, Miss Richards, the youngest patient admitted, is the daughter of a hospital director and one of the inpatients cared for by Dr. Schwartz.

The grandmother of one of Dr. Isaacson's outpatients is admitted and assigned to Dr. Augress. Mrs. Hammond has physical infirmities, and with belching, gobbling, and throaty half screams, she infuriates the nurses. They feel that attempts to "structure" her stay are undermined when her granddaughter calls Dr. Isaacson.

Mr. Phillips is a resourceful patient who steps into a breech. During February, while the therapists are feeling overworked and some nurses are consciously undermining Miss Conrad's authority, the patients form an unusually cohesive group under his leadership. Even the nursing staff shows a covert preference for his leadership. Much of his strength is in his subtle manipulation of people, persuading them to act on his own aggressive strivings for power.

Dr. Schwartz' patient, Mrs. Hecht, becomes another focus of the nurses malcontent. She cries out for help, especially at night, but when nurses come to her aid she rejects them, saying she can speak only to her therapist. At night she is typically found in disarray and her verbal accusations are experienced by the nurses as humiliating. The patient asks for, and is granted, permission not to be checked regularly during the night shift. The consensus among the nurses is disillusionment with Dr. Schwartz and Miss Conrad: with Dr. Schwartz for supposedly "favoring" the patient and with Miss Conrad for not supporting nursing and confronting the doctor.

On March 1, Miss Conrad goes on leave because of a real physical illness which has sapped her strength. On March 2, Mrs. Hecht is asked by Miss Serena for permission to use the bathtub in her room. The next day when the request is repeated Mrs. Hecht insults Miss Serena. The situation is loaded. Miss Siegel, with the covert support of nursing, denounces Mrs. Hecht for Miss Serena's "humiliation." The nurses who witness the episode "have had it." Mrs. Reilly confronts Mrs. Hecht, who goes into a rage.

On March 8 it is noted that Mrs. Hecht is eating very little, or not at all. She talks with Mrs. Reilly and complains that she is treated not as a patient, but somehow as a staff member. Mrs. Reilly relents and feeds her soup. The next day Mrs. Hecht packs all her belongings and puts them in the hall. Two days later Mrs. Hecht completely stops eating, and nursing finally confronts Dr. Schwartz over her physical needs. March 13 is the beginning of a week of tube feeding. Then all of nursing, including the aides, are assigned to administer food at intervals until the patient eats without assistance.

Clearly, the nursing staff trys to make amends in the face of guilt concerning Miss Conrad and Mrs. Hecht. Throughout this period the nurses experience frustrated negative and positive oedipal strivings.

On February 2, 1967 Miss Allen begins to participate in the mural sessions. Because her mural contributions will be taken up in some detail, it is important now to discuss Miss Allen herself. She is a bright and active, self-involved 18-year-old college freshman who is admitted in the aftermath of a legal abortion. She has expressed self-destructive feelings and the school psychiatrist advised hospitalization. The abortion culminated a long period of sexual acting out on the part of Miss Allen which her parents could not control. Athough talented and vivacious, Miss Allen would invariably find herself on the fringe of her peer group. She demanded attention by her willingness to act out sexually or with various psychedelic drugs. In the month prior to her hospitalization, she had three minor auto accidents. Her father is a hard-driving millionaire; her mother, a talented poet, albeit unstable and chronically dissatisfied. The parents had discussed and argued divorce as far back as the patient could remember. These plans are actually culminated during Miss Allen's stay on the ward. It becomes clear early in therapy that the acting out behavior serves to bring the parents together. The sexual promiscuity began early in adolescence when the patient felt that her father treated her in a markedly restricted and cool manner. On the one hand she was no longer his "little girl" but on the other, he would not allow her to be the sophisticate, which was the role of her older sister. Treatment is insight-oriented and designed to limit the acting out by appropriate interpretations. Miss Allen expresses considerable anger toward her father, at the same time that she engages in a mutually provocative relationship with him that constitutes unconscious behavior for both. She also expresses rage toward her mother, whom she felt abandoned her. She cannot forgive her mother for being so sick that the latter would become hysterical when Miss Allen needed her most. Predictably, all of these themes are enacted in the transference and played out with the other patients on the ward. The patient is discharged after six months with the intention of continuing college in the fall and resuming psychotherapy at that time. There is no indication of psychosis.

The next mural, beginning a new sequence, returns once again to the actual ward setting. The hellish mood also states the danger inherent in focusing power through one individual.

This is the showdown scene. The hour of judgment has arrived. Mrs. Polansky offers "matches" to light the flaming hell that is to be the theme of the mural. They call it "Herzl's Inferno" (#25), quite appropriately bringing the issues out into the open. This time they do not hide behind their carnival guises but show themselves as real people suffering the torments of their real experience. At the suggestion of "Herzl's Inferno," the patients' "concept of Hell," Miss Myers let it be known that the idea makes her feel like climbing the wall, by offering "Wall Climbing" as a theme. Mrs. Woodward wanted to go completely in the opposite direction, suggesting "Heaven" as an alternative. Following this a stream of avoidant themes is heard, such as "a ball, skiing and playground, golf course, a dress shop." Mrs. Woodward and Mrs. Weil suggest "a railroad station and a yacht," respectively. When the "Herzl's Inferno" theme is finally

Sequence V: Group Identification. Stages 1 & 2: Reality and Statement. "HERZL'S INFERNO," February 2, 1967, Mural #25.

chosen, Miss Meyers emphasizes her own and the group's excitement by wetting her pants. As Hell leaps into view with Mr. Wallace's and Miss Siegel's red and yellow flames, Mrs. Weil is very upset. She and Mrs. Woodward do not contribute anything to this mural. Neither for that matter does Mr. Phillips who sits this one out entirely in his isolated chair at the end of and behind the group. Clearly, he will play no active part in roasting Mr. Novick in Hell. It is equally clear that he will have no part in saving him. He sits as a silent observer, in the wings so to speak, awaiting the part he will play in due time. Miss Meyers decides to join in this game of the inferno by drawing a cartoon version of the devil with blue eyes resembling those of Mr. Novick. Miss Allen portrays herself as Tantalus with the receding water and unreachable grapes. Her chief concern is for her own inner needs. The extent to which they are unfulfilled is a measure of the depth of her private hell. Her other contributions include two people in a boat on the river Styx, lost souls in Purgatory, and St. Peter with a check list.

There is evidence of sexual byplay as the fires of Hell rage. Miss Meyers, angered by the implications of Mr. Novick's two large pitchforks, drawn at Miss Siegel's request, sketches her own red pitchfork and writes, "Husbands and wives. I've been there already. Sartre. Hell is other people." To demonstrate her awareness of what is going on, Miss Bernard adds fuel to the fire by drawing a baby devil.

With the heat of the moment increasing, Mr. Novick frantically attempts to discourage his would-be torturers. By introducing Einstein's mass-energy equation, he is warning them of the consequences of their intentions. He alludes to a Jewish name as familiar and as powerful as Herzl. By depicting Cerberus, he is associating himself with the omnipotent forces of Hell, unattainable and indestructible. Miss Bernard who at this point has had enough of Hell, draws a sign pointing upward reading, "Heaven directly upstairs." She offers this way of escape to all who would follow and leaves, in the figurative sense, as this is her final contribution to the mural.

In response to Miss Bernard's sign, the real Mr. Novick depicts himself crying, arms reaching heavenward in a desperate plea for salvation. To emphasize the futility of his gesture, Miss O'Rourke immediately draws a man upside down, his head stuck deep in the mud. The flow of tears represent Mr. Novick's painful realization of the passion with which his fellow patients desire his downfall. Determined to elude his fate, he draws a large dagger and writes "War" on Miss Allen's Tantalus, thus declaring his intention to fight off any attempts against him. Tauntingly, Miss Meyers writes, "What's cooking?"—an allusion to the mounting anger she senses is about to consume him. In one flaming last-ditch stand, he applies the red as a fiery torch to everyone's drawings, angrily crying out, "You want Hell? You've got it!" After this the group falls deathly silent.

Hell has frozen over in the "Winter Scene" (#26) of February 9th. In this mural, the subtle persecution of Mr. Novick begins. Mr. Phillips, the chief assassin, begins the discussion by suggesting, "Two snowmen, one representational and one way out." Seeing this picture more concretely as a contest between two men, Mr. Phillips is casting himself as the representational object, the true representative of the group. Mr. Novick, meanwhile, is being cast as the "way out" (crazy) man on his way out as leader of the group. Thus, one snowman is to represent a reality figure, while the other will be suitable for symbolic transformation. Miss Siegel expresses her own uncomfortable and reflective self-consciousness by suggesting "a mural of people doing a mural." Miss Bernard suggests a blizzard, the furious stuff out of which snow-

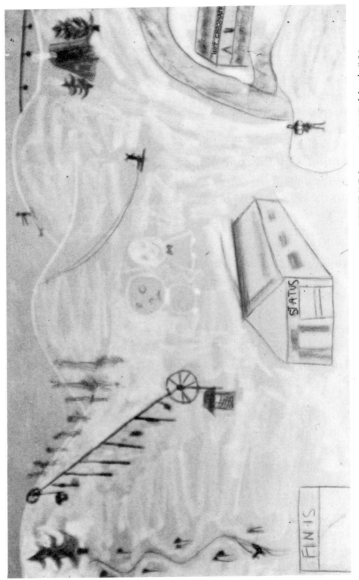

Sequence V: Group Identification. Stage 3: Defense. "WINTER SCENE," February 9, 1967, Mural #26.

men are made. Miss Bernard, preferring the earthly cold to the heat of last week's Hell, opens the door for another stormy scene. In that a snowman might be hard to find in a blizzard, her suggestion may also be seen as the expression of her ambivalence toward the dump-Novick movement. Mr. Novick's desperate attempt to reassert his leadership is put down as Miss Bernard tells him he's "not helping very much." Just as her attitude toward Miss Serena is divided, this statement has a two-part meaning. On the one hand, she is telling him to stop struggling and submit to execution. On the other, she is urging him to cooperate with her efforts to help him escape the group's wrath by lowering his visibility. In either case, his real power is ended. To emphasize this point Mr. Novick subjects himself to further humiliation by rushing to the panel to initiate the drawing of a skiing scene before the group has decided on a theme. By reminding him that he is still part of the group, the therapist seeks to rescue him from sudden annihilation and to maintain the process in its natural flow. To start, Mr. Perlin, Mr. Novick's crony, draws a "sad snowman." Mr. Novick draws a distant skier, and then another skier going through a difficult slalom course. Clearly, Mr. Novick is the sad figure of a snowman that tries to flee in and out of the encircling clutch of the group. Too late, he is turned to ice (depersonalized).

Miss Allen draws a hill with pine trees and a frame house also surrounded by trees. Her contribution is well neutralized, well structured, and nonrevealing. She is not yet ready to participate openly in an assassination. Other patients are equally evasive, stating their aversion to this mural. In this defensive mural, the process of making the group a mental representation of itself, a mural of a mural group's mind, is carried forward. Mr. Novick's image is to be assimilated and internalized.

The "Big Rock Candy Mountain" (#27) scene of the

following weeks is Miss Allen's choice. She draws the candy mountain with many sweets appended to it. The search for oral satiation recalls the girl Tantalus with grapes.

The group extends the design to incorporate Mr. Novick. A gingerbread man is the only representation of a human figure in the mural. Mr. Novick leaves. He returns during the discussion, just as Miss Hecht asks, "Is the person in the middle edible?" Seeing him, she adds, "Now we'll get some black," meaning literally that Mr. Novick will spread unwanted black on the mural, just as he had covered the "Hell" mural with red flames. The group asks him not to spoil it. He smiles and says that the mural takes him back to his childhood. Miss Hecht says, "The gingerman is central and smiling." Another patient says, "He seems to be attempting two smiles." This could refer to the two snowmen. The patient who drew the gingerbread man says, "If I had made him the way I felt, he wouldn't be too happy." Miss Hecht asks whether the mural is childish or childlike. This allusion to Mr. Novick's childhood remark clarifies an entire level of the conversation: that Mr. Novick is the edible gingerbread man, angrily trying to smile, while he should get his ginger up to "run, run, as fast as he can." At the end, Mr. Novick lamely tries to reassert his leadership by noting that the group has been rebelling. Although the dynamics are fairly clear, the patients' discussion and the mural itself still defensively avoid the murderous intent by emphasizing sweetness. The process of reducing Mr. Novick to an image of the group's self is continued.

"Mobile" (#28) on February 23 wins out over "Stabile," indicating, among other things, the movement toward the unconscious. The suggestions are made by Mr. Phillips, who is now rallying the group. There is a sense of fun as Mr. Phillips, taking an active lead, draws for the first time. When the group gathered itself for the session,

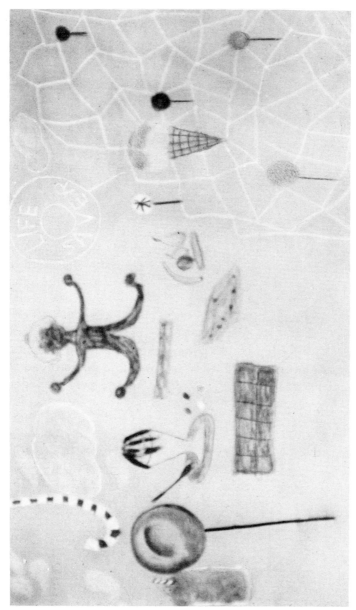

Sequence V: Group Identification. Stage 3: Defense. "BIG ROCK CANDY MOUNTAIN," February 16, 1967, Mural #27.

Sequence V: Group Identification. Stage 3: Defense. "MOBILE," February 23, 1967, Mural #28.

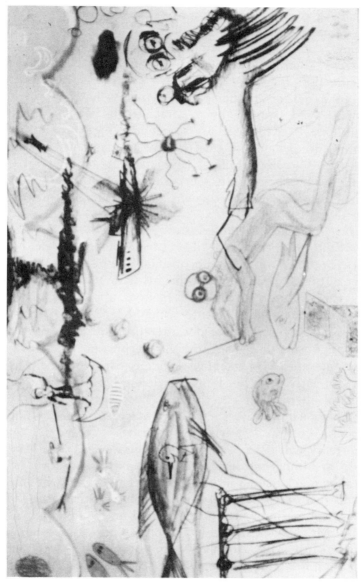

Sequence V: Group Identification. Stage 4: Unconscious. "A BEAUTIFUL UNDERWATER SCENE," March 2, 1967, Mural #29.

Miss Allen asked, "Where's Miss Hecht and Mrs. Weil?" Someone else said, "Mr. Phillips is playing chess in the living room." No one mentioned Mr. Novick.

Miss Allen draws a bird mobile, saying, "I draw what fits in, not what I feel." She also pronounces the mural completed after another patient remarks that a man who is portrayed hanging by a parachute is hanging by an umbilicus. Her remarks are somewhat enigmatic, but her future mural behavior reveals that she has developed an allegiance to Mr. Phillips, whom she treats as a rather privileged father figure. Certainly she approves of and participates vicariously in Mr. Phillips' displacement of Mr. Novick.

In "A Beautiful Underwater Scene" (#29) of March 2nd, the group ascribes all its own violence to Mr. Novick. In this mural of the unconscious, he becomes the carrier of their rage. The mural begins with Mr. Novick asking the patients to face their feelings about each other. He wants the anger out in the open. Mr. Perlin expresses anger at people who are not attending the mural, avoiding anger at those who are. Mr. Perlin and Mr. Novick compete openly to establish a theme. Mr. Novick tries to win an early vote, but he is put down. Mrs. Popidopolus' funeral theme loses to Mr. Phillips' suggestion of "A Beautiful Underwater Scene." Mr. Novick starts with a large fish on the left. Miss Allen draws a yellow fish that she fears will be eaten by Mr. Novick's fish. She wants help in hiding hers. Mr. Novick's next contribution is a strange black man, a motif inappropriate to the swans and small fish drawn by the others. Then he sketches a Japanese submarine which is being fired on by a plane. Next time, Mr. Novick draws heavy black lines to accentuate and enclose Miss Allen's "Venus on a Shell," thus enveloping her. He then depicts an atomic explosion. A patient remarks, "This was supposed to be calm."

Miss Allen remarks that the Venus inscribed on a sea

shell looks like a girl popping out of a cake. In the dynamics of the group's interaction, she is telling Mr. Phillips that if he saves her from Mr. Novick's enveloping clutches, he can have her sexually. She draws a chest of gold on the sea bottom, further emphasizing her value.

Another patient reminds Mrs. Popidopolus of her intent to draw a coffin. The wish to kill Mr. Novick is now present. Mrs. Popidopolus answers that Miss Hecht's swan is roasted now. Miss Hecht says, "You wanted a funeral." At this point the dynamics of the entire ward are being enacted with considerable individual variation. Miss Hecht, Dr. Schwartz' representative in the patient group, feels under attack and she is about to undergo decompensation. Miss Conrad, the Head Nurse, has actually been under attack, having developed a physical sickness, and Dr. Schwartz is himself under fire. Miss Allen's feeling of sexual affiliation to Mr. Phillips also reflects the ward's rampant oedipal dynamic.

In the discussion, Mr. Phillips maintains that "Underwater Scene" was a unified theme except for Mr. Novick's angry expressions. Mrs. Popidopolus adds that Mr. Novick's violent contributions were unnecessary. Mr. Novick argues. The group agrees that Mr. Novick is a bad, destructive man.

The therapist asks how the group feels about Mr. Phillips' lack of graphic contributions. Mr. Phillips says, "Stop riding me and get back to Mr. Novick." Clearly, Mr. Novick wants to devour the group and destroy it. However, the group, led by Mr. Phillips, is in control. Actually, they are doing a kind of violence to Mr. Novick, while proclaiming their innocence. In a way each group member has become an individual purveyor of violence.

Mr. Phillips and Mrs. Popidopolus, who are most instrumental in this mural, are both recovering from psychotic depressive episodes. Their therapist, Dr. Lukens, is

portrayed as the victim in subsequent murals. This mural
of the unconscious reflects structural transformation as
Mr. Novick's image is internalized and thereafter suitable
for transmitting the group's sense of strength. Mr. Phillips presents the external form of this image.

On March 9 the theme "Fence" (#30) is suggested by
Mr. Phillips. Other suggestions are "Tombstones for the
Doctors" and "Shit on Shit." Mr. Phillips, Mrs. Popidopolus and Miss Allen, Dr. Lukens' patients, are joined
by Mr. Novick in expressing themes of overt hostility.
Mrs. Popidopolus draws a gingerbread house and Mr.
Novick says, "Nice house." Mr. Novick draws a man
hanging from a tree and a bullet's trajectory through
the head of a male figure.

Miss Allen writes "shit" on the fence, a bicycle outside
the fence, followed by a heart enclosing the names "David
& Lisa." Another patient had associated her name in a
heart with that of Mr. Perlin. She obliterates this. Then
she writes "fuck" on the fence. Next she draws a red
car outside the fence. Finally, she draws green grass
and a weeping willow tree in the enclosure next to Mr.
Phillips' drawing of a house, and a "wicked old witch"
at some distance from this house. This mural yields a
striking example of the way in which an individual with
an intact ego can utilize the available symbolism. The
aspect of acting out excites her own inclination to do
so to wit, the unleashing of written obscenities and the
depiction of sexual symbols. The latter appear outside
the fence, that is, outside of control. This configuration
matches her character structure which is outwardly rebellious, both sexually and aggressively. Inside the fence,
a weeping willow tree, close to the house of Mr. Phillips,
and a wicked old witch, complete the picture. She weeps
at the futility of her attempt to get close to her father
while wanting to kill the wicked old mother. These
oedipal themes are repeatedly expressed in her psycho-

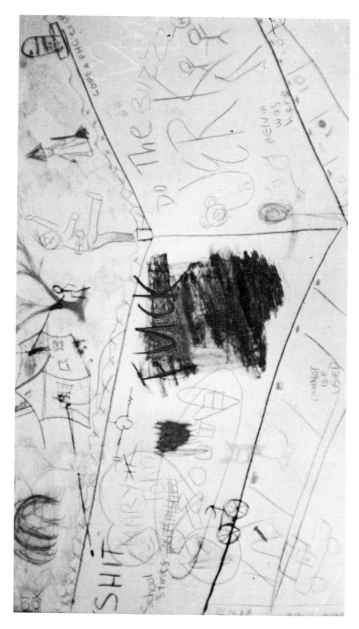

Sequence V: Group Identification. Stage 5: Recombination. "FENCE," March 9, 1967, Mural #30.

therapy. Miss Allen is able to utilize the structure of the mural to reflect different aspects of herself. Thus the fence is a boundary upon which and outside of which her character may be revealed, while her wishes and fantasies are portrayed as an inner core.

Mr. Phillips begins the discussion by saying that "gingerbread" refers to Mr. Novick's rage. It may be recalled that Mr. Novick was the gingerbread man in "Big Rock Candy Mountain," (#27). Then Mrs. Popidopolus, referring to the staff, says that she only wishes them dead. The group agrees that the mural represents feelings about the ward. Mr. Novick claims that the doctors will get more out of the mural than a "nice picture." Miss Hecht tells him to "stop pontificating." Mr. Novick's position has changed from the displaced object of aggression to the vehicle for rage. He actually embodies the patients' rage as it is now directed outward to the staff, especially to the doctors. When the members of the group attempted to extrude Mr. Novick, they were trying to isolate their own rage. The change in Mr. Novick's status reflects the recombination stage of the sequence.

In the "French Revolution" (#31) mural of March 16, the theme of ritual killing is enacted. Although Mr. Phillips wants to add the words "with guillotine" to the title, he states that he isn't participating because he doesn't approve of the theme. Actually, he directs Mrs. Popidopolus, Miss Allen and Mr. Novick in the macabre ceremony.

Mr. Novick makes an early bid to take control of the mural group rather than be controlled by it and be subjected to the execution he senses is in store for him. It is precisely at Mrs. Popidopolus' suggestion, "Let's have a planned murder and mayhem. Let's organize it," that Mr. Novick leaps to his feet to proclaim himself a "natural leader." By shouting him down, they serve notice once

Sequence V: Group Identification. Stages 5 & 6: Recombination & Resolution. "FRENCH REVOLUTION," March 16, 1970, Mural #31.

and for all that he is to be deposed and made subject to the will of the group. In one last defiant effort to at least determine his own execution and steal the play from the group, he draws a guillotine with a decapitated head (his) and a bucket to catch it in. By actively deposing himself, Mr. Novick paves the way to a sense of his own identification with the other group members. It is Mr. Novick who portrays Dr. Lukens as Hitler watching the proceedings. During the mural, Mr. Novick bemoans three brothers fighting in Vietnam. He states his fear of being torn apart, but there is no sympathy.

Miss Allen, as the active henchwoman of Mr. Phillips, draws the road, a spectator, Madame Defarge, knitting, and Marie Antoinette riding in a cart. Mr. Novick writes, "SHIT" in capital letters which Miss Allen transforms into four figures on the way to the guillotine. She adds the tricolor and Viva France. After all this activity she comments that it is hard to be involved. The murder of Mr. Novick, the Chief Doctor, the Head Nurse, Dr. Lukens and Miss Hecht are probably all implicit. It is noteworthy that all the active participants in the mural are patients of Dr. Lukens.

To begin the discussion, Mr. Phillips puns, "Well executed." Mr. Perlin follows, "It's revolting." After Mr. Novick expresses further fears for his family, Mr. Phillips comments that the head in the basket is smiling. Mr. Novick is clearly an instrument of the group's sadism. The shift in Mr. Novick's structural position in the group, from an object or target to a subject who expresses anger for the group, reveals a true internalization. In abstract terms, an object image has been incorporated into the self with a corresponding shift in dynamics such that aggression that was bound in the object's image is now available for the self's (group) disposition.

As a background to this mural of resolution, it is noted that Miss Hecht is now being "saved by tube feeding."

Sequence V: Group Identification. Stage 6: Resolution. "OPERATING ROOM," March 23, 1967, Mural #32.

This involves a coming together of the staff in a spirit of cooperation, which successfully overcomes the murderous antagonisms of recent weeks. Dr. Schwartz is restored to grace as his patient receives treatment, the nurses are unified and the patients reflect the dynamics in the mural.

As the patients enter the room, their facial expressions are a mixture of abject concern and intense thoughtfulness. An air of depression and tension pervades the room. There is a long moment of silence before one of them, Miss Richards, speaks.

Miss Richards: "Who has an idea?"

Mr. Phillips: "How about an operating scene?" This suggestion stirs the group. Bowed heads are raised followed by nodding and verbal approval. Mr. Phillips' idea for the mural's theme is unanimously accepted.

Miss Richards: "It will need a circle—looking down."

Mr. Phillips: "To create tension we need tension."

Miss Allen: "Mr. Novick is going to do guts and everything."

Mr. Phillips: "Now we'll see where anxiety sets in. Let's get started."

At this point, two of the patients, Mrs. Klein and Miss Meyers, leave the room. Mr. Perlin follows, announcing his intention to bring Miss Meyers back.

Miss Richards—draws an operating table with a patient on it.

Miss Allen attempts to draw a stand with equipment for intravenous treatment.

Miss Richards draws a pink machinelike object attached to the leg.

Mr. Phillips draws an anesthesia machine.

Miss Richards draws a hole in the patient's stomach to show the machine's attachment to the insides.

Miss Allen contributes a tile floor.

Mr. Phillips draws two doctors looking down on a patient. He states, "No one has established a sex yet for the patient. Why are we avoiding that?" This is said with an air of sarcasm. He then proceeds to draw an African witch doctor. He asks Mr. Novick to complete the drawing.

Mr. Novick obliges.

Miss Richards draws a laser beam and adds more people watching the operation.

Mr. Perlin draws a boxlike object.

Mr. Phillips asks, "Which doctor's name are we going to put on the patient?"

Miss Richards: "Not Dr. Schwartz because he's a teddy bear." She then draws a teddy bear.

Miss Allen: "Let's make a nurse who faints during the operation."

Mr. Novick draws blood "gushing out" of the patient.

Miss Richards draws a bucket full of vital organs.

Mr. Novick: "We can't put hair on his head because he's having brain surgery too."

Miss Richards: "He also has gangrene and leprosy of the foot."

Mr. Phillips: "See folks, when we start early, we can get much more cooperation."

Mr. Novick labels the patient "Dr. Lukens."

Mrs. Popidopolus: "Not even I wish him that. Why, he's your doctor too, Mr. Phillips."

Miss Allen contributes a blood bank while commenting, "Poor Dr. Lukens, why pick on him?"

Miss Richards draws a little girl with a balloon looking away from the operation.

Mr. Phillips: "Draw a TV set with Ben Casey on it."

Miss Richards complies with Mr. Phillips' request.

Mrs. Popidopolus draws an angel of mercy.

Mr. Novick to Mrs. Popidopolus: "You changed your mind since last week."

Mrs. Popidopolus: "I know more now."

Miss Richards contributes a jar of blood.

Miss Richards and Miss Allen both draw flowers.

Mr. Phillips: "I want to prove to the doctors that I don't have color shock." He colors in a polygraph with orange.

Mr. Novick adds an arm band with a swastika on it.

The group shouts its objection to the suggestion of politics or religion.

Miss Richards and Miss Allen return to their drawings of flowers.

Mr. Novick adds sutures and bloody gangrene to the patient.

Mr. Phillips: "Draw a Rabbi reading the good book. You do it, Mr. Glick." There is no response from Mr. Glick, an orthodox Jew, even though Mr. Phillips is very much in control of the group.

Mrs. Popidopolus: "Don't do anything to my angel."

Miss Allen: "We really need a Rabbi."

Miss Richards draws a Rabbi, while Mr. Glick watches intently. She asks, "How do you write Hebrew? Mine would look like Chinese."

Miss Allen: "Since we have a Rabbi, we're going to need a Priest. And we should give him a cross. Then we'll also need a Minister."

There is a period of silence and a pause in activity as they survey the mural. Mr. Novick's statement, "There's not enough blood," signals the beginning of a discussion of the mural.

Mr. Phillips: "Is this patient going to survive? Can we let Dr. Lukens die?"

Mrs. Popidopolus: "I could have saved myself the trouble. I drew an angel of mercy up there. He never needed all that crap."

Miss Richards insists that he'll be reincarnated.

Miss Allen: "I don't think it should be Dr. Lukens."

Mrs. Popidopolus: "Me either." She gets up and crosses off his name.

Miss Allen: "Why don't we just call him Dr. 'X'?"

Mr. Novick objects to Mrs. Popidopolus' crossing out of Dr. Lukens' name.

Mrs. Popidopolus: "Can't we make it the Universal sick me?"

Mr. Phillips checks with the recorder, Miss Callahan, as to whether she had recorded the writing of Dr. Lukens' name on the patient. Assured that she had, he then asked the group, "Can anyone draw a soul arising from the body?"

Mr. Foley responds by drawing a red and black smoke-like figure.

Mrs. Popidopolus: "That's the sick me going out of the body."

Miss Richards: "We should have a white one too."

Mr. Foley: "Just a shadow of it."

The group, not too pleased with the goriness of the scene, is approving of Miss Allen's suggestion stated as a question. She asks, "Can't we do, after he gets to heaven in next week's mural?"

Miss Richards suggests that each member of the group relate what the patient depicted in the mural symbolizes to him or her.

Mr. Phillips offers a tongue-in-cheek comment on the group's cooperation.

Miss Richards observes that each one felt differently. "Some like destroyers, some like healers."

Miss Allen disagrees. "I'm neither."

Mr. Phillips states that he "hopes the group didn't feel coerced" by his encouragement to get started. The group denied feeling coerced and agreed that his suggestion helped to save time.

Miss Richards and Mrs. Popidopolus argue as to the identity of the patient in the mural.

Mrs. Popidopolus: "It's the sick me, not someone else."

Miss Richards: "It's really Dr. Lukens. He survives, but he has to be tortured."

Mr. Foley draws a dagger in the heart.

The therapist, Mr. Blackman, questions whether the mural is the group's or Mr. Phillips'. There is no response. He asks if it is an "angry" mural.

Miss Allen denies that it is an "angry" mural.

Mr. Novick and Miss Richards differ with Miss Allen. They agree with each other that the mural is an expression of anger.

Mr. Phillips expresses doubt and will not commit himself.

Miss Richards: "It's like being involved in a killing. Makes you feel guilty and bad. I want to save the victim."

Mr. Novick: "It could be sickness we're trying to kill. But there's that angel up there wanting sickness to be saved."

Through guilt, the group's final resolution is to transfer the aggression from the object to the "bad self," then by exorcising the bad self the aggression can be averted.

This mural is the last of a long series of sadistic attacks on Mr. Novick and other hapless leaders. It re-emerges toward the ward's reality as Dr. Lukens is depicted as the victim. The group can avoid for the moment having its cohesion ripped apart by directing hostility toward the real figure of Dr. Lukens who has been treating the protagonists. Dr. Lukens also serves as a displacement figure for Dr. Schwartz, who was first mentioned as the potential victim. During the past weeks both doctors had received considerable opposition from the staff over their permissive handling of their patients. The onset of the attempt to "save" the victim marks a shift in the group's method of handling its aggression. There are elements of preparation for the group's "totem feast" of the succeeding mural, as Miss Richards depicts Dr. Schwartz as her Teddy Bear and Dr. Lukens' insides are laid open for the group's upcoming internalization feast.

Sequence VI: Group Guilt (3/30/67–4/20/67)

The group abandons itself to the ravages of its new hippy-cultist leader in April. Mr. Foley is a psychedelic giant—a tall, dark, bearded, long-haired, gentle savage. Heir, among patients, to Mr. Phillips, he becomes an object of love for several patients, male and female, and possibly for one member of the nursing staff.

From the time of his admission, he is "different." His orders include permission to allow him to leave the ward when he feels uncontrollable and anxious. He was trained in judo. No one is able to control him. He can't control himself. His therapist, Dr. Augress, can't.

The inability to deal with Mr. Foley reflects the ongoing dynamics of the ward. His admission forces the worried reappearance of Dr. Isaacson onto the ward scene. Still acting as Dr. Isaacson's therapeutic right hand, Dr. Augress is given the task of treating Mr. Foley for his decompensating, borderline condition. At this time the individual doctors feel guilty as they operate in their own spheres and the nursing staff feels guilty, having "rid" itself of Miss Conrad's control. When Miss Conrad became ill, the nursing staff seemed relieved and assumed the example of her assistant. However, discipline diminishes among patients and staff. Miss Marsh, who is given to "mothering," has been able to work very well with individual patients and is trusted by the long-term patients. However, she is not a talented administrator, a failing which is compounded by the fact that it is not clear how long the Head Nurse will be absent. Even her role as an able nurse is in the process of being eclipsed by a new nurse, Miss Salvatore. Miss Marsh's leadership is questioned by nursing. The bickering is brought into the open at the end of April. Staff tells her to lead and to stop waiting for Miss Conrad's return. The nursing staff falls into a kind of disarray in April. During this period, three adolescents are admitted who are depressed and suicidal.

The "Zoo" (#33) mural of March 30 initiates a new sequence. This mural has a cannibalistic theme, i.e., eating the dead leader in order to incorporate his identity. By participating in the celebration, each animal emerges equally as the leader. This mural combines the first two stages of a sequence while it demonstrates, nonpareil, the previous resolution. It depicts the patients in full animal regalia, while a game that is played during the discussion—"What kind of animal would you like to be?"—reveals that the animal form is a disguise. "Zoo" is the culmination of a long symbolic process of overthrowing the leader by depicting a ritual Totem Feast. In that the theme is so reminiscent of Freud's (1913) reconstruction of the fantasy underlying *Totem and Taboo,* the mural will be described in some detail. In a later chapter this material will be used to elaborate on Freud's conclusions in *Totem and Taboo.*

Miss Allen begins the theme discussion by saying, "Whatever John wants." John Phillips had established himself in the last sequence as the heroic leader of the revolution to oust Mr. Novick. Miss Allen now worships him.

Mr. Phillips responds, "A Banquet Scene." This initial presentation is focal, containing the spirit of celebration and incorporation which is his to impart.

Miss Allen answers, "Last Supper." In perfect harmony she carries the theme back to the dead leader, bringing in the religious symbolism of the eating of Christ's flesh.

Rosa Richards, Dr. Schwartz's presently adoring young patient, adds, "Easter." This note of resurrection is reminiscent of the attempt last week to "raise" the dying Doctor Lukens. It carries the theme forward toward an incorporation of the spirit of the glorified dead leader.

A young adolescent girl, fearful of the ravenous group, suggests, "Disneyland." Sensing her fear of hostility, Mr. Phillips says, "There should be no hostility." To prove it he demands, "Go get Uncle Paul."

Mr. Novick, thus referred to, has been detained in his entrance to the mural session. Mr. Phillips, beyond the gratuitous allusion to Mr. Novick's absence, is announcing that the latter's image should enter into the theme discussion. He suggests "Sculpture Garden." This brings the group further toward its present scene than does Disneyland and it brings the essence of the dead figure of Mr. Novick closer to a symbolic form of incarnation.

Rosa, slipping back to the past and unable to fully neutralize her aggression, suggests "Revolution." But Miss Allen picks up the garden theme, saying, "Flowers. No people in it." Rosa carries the trend to its conclusion with "Zoo."

As Miss Allen and Rosa rise to plan the spacing for the zoo, Mr. Novick enters, miffed that the theme selection has gone along without him.

Rosa declares, "Let's put the people on the inside of the cages and the animals on the outside." Humorous and defiant, her remark also promotes the idea of incorporation. Confirming that the patients are the animal figures incorporating their objects, she proceeds to draw a lion, labelling it "Dr. Schwartz."

The young adolescent girl, still fearing the hostility of "sick" or "bad" patients, draws a "healthy giraffe."

A new adolescent woman, also wanting to stay above it all but entering the group spirit of usurping an identity, says, "I'm stealing this activity for when I go back to work."

Miss Allen draws a duckbilled platypus, i.e., something which is one thing at the mouth and something else in the body.

Fred, a naive and new adolescent, is unable to disguise the activity sufficiently as he draws a "blue two-legged animal."

Mrs. Popidopolus, a mainstay of the last sequence, draws a "five-legged hyena eating a man." With this she fully introduces the banquet theme of incorporation.

Rosa draws a "pigeon-toed pigeon." With this peer encouragement pointing the way toward combining human and animal characteristics, the adolescent girl draws "a giant lady bug."

Rosa says, "I'll make a man bug."

A moment later Mrs. Hecht, also a patient of Dr. Schwartz, notices Rosa's lion. Rosa offers a portion saying, "We share!" At this Mrs. Hecht says, "I have to add something," and possessively, she presents the lion with a scarf. "Be careful!" warns Rosa.

After an interchange between Miss Allen and Mrs. Hecht, which centers on the degree of maleness of the former's fat orangutan and on the nature of the "weird disease" displayed by her green-spotted giraffe, she suggests, "Let's bring in a doctor."

Mr. Novick springs to his feet.

"No swastikas," a group member says.

He draws a pennant inscribed, "Strange Animals often Fall out." This may allude to Dr. Lukens' demise, to his own ostracism and indirectly to the fate of sick animals. At this point Miss Allen brings in her formal and stiff doctor Lukens by drawing a "penguin in a tuxedo."

Now Rosa asks if she can draw spots on Miss Hecht's elephant. This is a threat to make Miss Hecht sick because she is seen as an elephant in the competition for Dr. Schwartz. But is it Dr. Schwartz who is the elephant. Miss Hecht chooses to think so, answering, "Go ahead, he's mine." Ambiguity is available as humor because the percipient can choose to identify with the internalized object or with the self.

Sequence IV: Group Guilt. Stages 1 & 2: Reality and Statement. "ZOO," March 30, 1967, Mural #33.

Rosa asks, "Can I make someone sitting on him?"

Mr. Phillips, catching on, draws an owl. He knows the women are competing for possession of the man and suddenly he is the man. "John is the wise owl," Rosa says.

This brings an interlude of sweet feminine participation, butterflies, milk, a blonde girl.

Mr. Phillips says, "There are no reptiles." Rosa and Miss Hecht, still competing, draw snakes.

Then Rosa, to leave no doubt, outlines her lion in green, commenting that "it means jealousy."

The adolescent girl says that the mural needs a "purple people-eater."

Rosa draws it, returns from the board, and sits in Mrs. Hecht's lap. This act reduces the tension and competition. After all there is enough sustenance for everyone. The group can begin its discussion in a pleased fashion.

The mural receives admiration. Fred emphasizes that there is no violence.

Mrs. Papidopolus says, "a little."

Miss Hecht, taking the cue, points out, "Paul didn't do anything."

Then they attempt to name the mural: "Saturday at the Zoo"—"Sunday at the Zoo"—"Who's Who at the Zoo." Mr. Novick tries to intrude, "Who's Who on 12-N." He is shouted down, easily, Two older patients want to leave at this outbreak of manifest violence. But Mr. Novick questions, "Which animal would each person like to be?"

Rosa says quickly, "Dr. Schwartz."

Mr. Phillips chooses his owl.

Rosa objects, "Each person will choose what they have drawn."

But Miss Hecht chooses Mr. Phillips' owl, confirming once again the competitive identification with the leader. Predictably Mr. Novick chooses the tiger, Mrs. Popidopolus, the man-eating hyena, Miss Allen, her penguin-doctor. The flighty adolesent girl chooses a bird, specifically a dove of peace. With this last break in the tension, the group can end the activity.

It is notable that each transition to a new phase of the mural activity occurs with a drop in tension induced by a reduction in hostility. Indeed, the whole mural of incorporation, identification and internalization serves to bind the members' hostility. With the hostility under control, the members can elaborate their new identity elements with fine-flowing expression. Seen as a whole the mural is luxurious. Identity proliferates in profuse, vivid forms and colors.

By April 6, Mr. Foley has suffused the world of 12-N. In his explosive unpredictability he has shattered the seclusion room, flaying the plaster from the walls. Mr. Phillips is soon to be discharged; Mr. Novick is missing.

The group faces the "End of the World" (#34) without a protector. Mrs. Popidopolus had suggested the theme of "12-N, a Self-Portrait," implicitly acknowledging that the group has a self. The "End of the World" theme expresses the "self" in a state of explosion. In the mural, Rosa draws a dominant, impassive, God-like face, protruding from a bomb blast. One patient claims, "God, or someone in the sky, is watching." Another says, "Someone from the next world is watching the destruction of this one." The group-self is now watching in detached horror. The vision of another world to come is implemented by the gradual addition of religious symbols.

Miss Allen draws the sun, "all old and dying," a volcano, burning trees and a house on fire. She asks another patient to draw people jumping out of windows. The group's excitement carries her into her own realm of action. She depicts an unprotected scene of mass destruction and the wish to flee, albeit self-destructively.

In the mural, the group expresses a more malignant

Sequence VI: Group Guilt. Stage 3: Defense. "END OF THE WORLD," April 6, 1967, Mural #34.

form of defensive flight. In the face of an overwhelming threat, i.e., Mr. Foley's destructive rage, and having left itself vulnerable by getting rid of prior dominant leaders, the group abandons itself to a violent shudder of self-annihilation. It is apparently preferable to destroy oneself than to be destroyed. The postmural discussion ends when a group member suggests that there will be only one survivor, presumably Mr. Foley.

In the "Emotions" (#35) mural of April 13, the unconscious is depicted, not with the previous land/water demarcations, but as the realm of pure feeling using "Emotions," rather than an externalized symbol reflects the groups heightened sense of itself as an entity. The group expresses feelings of impotent rage and of unprotected vulnerability.

It dramatizes the destruction of the body of the self. Castration is exemplified as Mr. Phillips draws a man with a hole in his chest and his heart in his hand. Green snakes, bleeding hearts, disembodied eyes and penis, and severed breasts complete a picture of castration and finally of bodily disintegration. Anger yields to resignation, and resignation is replaced by a feeling of desertion. "How do you draw the tit that wasn't there?" one patient asks. A quiet attempt to scapegoat Mr. Novick is drowned in a chorus of motherless wails. Miss Allen excitedly accuses Miss Callahan, a mother figure, of not liking her.

Miss Allen draws a black spot; a head filled with different colors which she refers to as a mixed bag of tantrum, envy and rage; and a flowerlike, so-called happiness figure protruding into nothingness. She also sketches a green-eyed monster to portray envy.

Mr. Novick draws a large red tearing eye, affixing "God Help Me" to it. Someone draws a penis discharging into the eye. Then Miss Allen says that someone should put something in nothing, a sexual reference. Mr. Novick

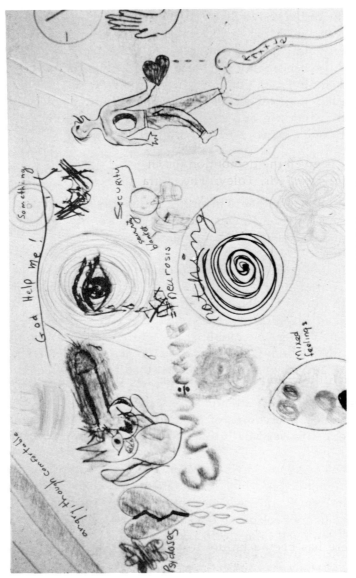

Sequence VI: Group Guilt. Stage 4: Unconscious. "EMOTIONS," April 13, 1967, Mural #35.

then announces that Mr. Phillips should put a big penis in the middle of his man with the hole in his chest. The castration scene is consummated as Mr. Foley finally enters the mural room, commenting that Mr. Novick is trying to take Mr. Phillips' place. That is Mr. Foley's signal that he is himself taking over.

The "Doctors and Patients" (#36) mural of April 20 demonstrates a resolution in which the fragmented group allows itself to be overwhelmed and victimized. Mr. Novick is given the demolition job in lieu of an even greater threat from Mr. Foley. The mural portrays a symbolic castration of the doctors.

Mr. Novick draws castrated and debunked caricatures of Dr. Augress, his therapist, and of Dr. Lukens. The group passively acquiesces to his cartoon. The mural expresses its grievance with the male objects who have failed to supply adequate protection. Miss Allen misses the mural session, but Mr. Ronan, who takes an active part in subsequent murals, makes his debut. He objects to the defiling of his doctor and he argues with Mr. Novick about whether doctors are good or evil. This mural has a cartoon quality which expresses the loss of vitality which the group has undergone. The distinction between the internalized object and the self is about to begin blurring.

Sequence VII: Group Regression (4/27/67—6/14/67).

The period of marked group regression extends through May and most of June. An increasing sense of isolation and loneliness pervades the unit, fostering a receptivity to mother figures.

In early May a "Communication Book" is established. There has been a failure to communicate pertinent data, policy changes, observations of patients' behavior, etc. to the various shifts. The Activity Staff's separation from

Sequence VI: Group Guilt. Stages 5 & 6: Recombination and Resolution. "DOCTORS AND PATIENTS," April 20, 1967, Mural #36.

Nursing Staff is open and hostile. The lack of rapport between physicians and nursing increases with a growing work load. The large staff of nurses and aides becomes increasingly divergent as several staff members continue their postgraduate education.

The "Communication Book" becomes the vehicle for exposing anger and frustration. Complaints and arguments are now recorded whereas previously disagreeing parties engaged in direct confrontation. Even when new procedures or policies are presented there are written debates and criticisms. Thus the "Communication Book" becomes a barometer of staff regression as the "ward" is treated as if it were a thing or object.

Two patients admitted in May create changes in the type of care that nursing is able or willing to give. Miss Jacobs, a wealthy girl, whose first hospitalization was at a well-known, well structured institution, is admitted for a therapeutic abortion. Her hospitalization is extended. Nursing feels that structure is required for her, particularly when she smokes marijuana on the unit. Miss Jacobs, who attracts male patients, has elicited concern from Mr. Foley, who regards her with extreme gentleness.

Miss Selig, a severely regressed schizophrenic adolescent girl, is admitted for a potentially long stay. Her hospitalization is paid for by her father's very substantial civil service insurance. Most of the time she actively hallucinates. She is "in love" with two of the Beatles. She ignores the rules of personal hygiene, particularly at the time of her menses. Dr. Augress is questioned by staff whether psychotherapy can help this patient. Miss Selig is in need of a strongly structured environment to keep clean, clothed and limited in her food intake. She cannot live in a room with another person. A nursing aide is assigned to work with her.

The month of May continues to be one of crisis. Mr.

Novick admits that he is back on his drug and blames his "fall" on the lack of support from the staff. Dr. Augress is blamed by nursing. Mr. Foley submits a letter of discharge and becomes a day patient. His time on the unit is spent sleeping.

One of the first admissions, Miss Bernard, is working part-time as a typist, although she requires enormous support to simply get herself going in the morning. Nursing grudgingly keeps her company while she breakfasts. Mr. Gordon, the Psychiatric Social Worker, organizes patient meetings. Most of the complaints come from patients, such as Miss Bernard, who are working and/or have been hospitalized for some time. It is decided that Miss Marsh will conduct a group for outgoing patients, which ultimately becomes a bridge between the experience of the hospital and the outside world. The atmosphere of the unit alternates between conflict and lethargy. Doctors give passes without defining the time limit; patients ignore the defined time once it is imposed. Beds go unmade for days. The eating areas become strewn with dirty dishes and left-over snacks. Patients admit smoking marijuana on and off the ward. When Mr. Gordon discusses patients' responsibilities, most patients flatly state that they just don't care.

Finally, on June 6th, a nursing staff meeting is held during which the need for strong leadership is angrily voiced. In order to help Miss Marsh strengthen her administrative role, Miss Salvatore is elected to function as her assistant. A financial secretary is appointed to reorganize the billing system. The third step in putting the house in order is the hiring of a receptionist. Mrs. Brown's job is to supervise the door which, being open eight hours, constitutes an "open unit" on 12-N. By virtue of her warmth and personality her role is extended to include other functions. The front door gradually becomes a focal point for the younger patients and the beginning of a compact adolescent group. They sit there talking and listening to music from the nearby record room, often expressing more of their feelings to the receptionist than to the professional staff. Mrs. Brown receives the outpatients as they come for their appointments and becomes a liaison between the inpatient and outpatient services. She also serves as a gentle sounding board for members of staff who congregate at the open door in an effort to escape, at least temporarily, the pressures in the nursing station.

Thus, the increasing regression and disorganization is resolved through acquisition of a number of maternal figures. May and June are the era of Miss Salvatore. She leads nursing in the tightening of controls and offers time and attention to the patients' needs. The patients vie for individual attention and demand constant mothering. After the discharge of Miss Allen, Miss Salvatore becomes the mothering leader whose time is consumed by the patients who rely on her to express their feelings. She takes over the unit, overstepping the Assistant Head Nurse and the seniority of other staff nurses. She is permissive but structured. By the end of June she is engaged to be married. As her time of departure becomes imminent, she makes herself even more indispensable. Finally, there is resentment. How can a "mother" of perfect empathy abandon her children?

Mr. Ronan is a new psychotic member of an increasingly psychotic and adolescent assemblage. Folk rock is the echoing heartbeat of the unit from morning until night. Bob Ronan is a grandiose 18-year-old college student who is admitted after taking an overdose of aspirin. Prior to his transfer to 12-N he had spent a month at another hospital. The suicide attempt was precipitated by an overwhelming sense of anger toward his 24-year-old brother. Living with his brother and mother in a small apartment, he would lie awake at night listening to the pacing footsteps of his brother, fearing that the latter would enter his room, or perhaps even worse, go into the mother's room. The father's death when the patient was seven, created a living legend which permeated the lives of the three remaining family members.

Mr. Ronan has a markedly perfectionistic sense of his own person. His gestures are exemplary, if not effeminate. Every movement is a study. His behavior alternates between sharp, piercing and sarcastic attacks on the hapless members of the patient group, and peculiar, infantile entreaties for help. He experiences the stigmata of his psychosis in a feeling of bodily detachment, and in the sense of a lovely princess whom he feels inhabits him. At the age of 10, he had experienced auditory hallucinations. He dreams of the inevitable "thin man" who will spread his evil influence everywhere. In his psychotherapy, Mr. Ronan constantly enacts the role of one or another family member, never himself.

This sequence begins with a mural the sentiment of which suggests a signpost—to the lost traveler in a strange country. The reality scene is now the "body" of the group. The disruption of the body integrity of the group-self is confirmed when Mrs. Popidopolus suggests, "a combination of us in a body." Miss Allen answers, "You'll only get a mass obscenity." "Maybe I want to show that I feel obscene inside," is the reply. Miss Richards says, "That's very confused speech, inside and outside of people." Mr. Novick says, "Let's draw the in between, inside yourself and outside in your mask." Miss Allen suggests "Abstract Art." Mr. Perlin says, "I want that, too." Mrs. Popidopolos declares angrily, "I'm surprised to hear that from you. You're always hiding in your shell."

Throughout the execution of "Abstract" (#37), pa-

Sequence VII: Group Regression. Stage 1: Reality. "ABSTRACT," April 27, 1967, Mural #37.

tients complain that they feel a lack of unit. A heart and bones, and a stick figure, amid the other fragments, provide a mere skeleton for the group. In depicting the group's loss of bodily substance and image, this mural fulfills the threat of castration that emerged in the previous session.

Miss Allen draws a series of squares followed by a stick-figure sculpture. Her stick figures lend more body structure than others can contribute. Mr. Ronan writes "Campbell Soup." This is a concrete reference to the Warhol painting. He treats the words as if they were the image. Then he draws two faces, one of which appears in a mirror. He draws a heart over another person's drawing. Mr. Ronan's imagery in this mural is consistent with the group's mixed-up body. The drawing of a heart separate but connected to another person's contribution depicts his inability to join his feelings with his own body. The mirror-image faces are a favorite mode of representation for him. Conceivably, this reflects his inability to differentiate between self and object in his own mental structure.

The mural of May 4, entitled "Jungle," (#38) is the group's statement of its attempt to find representation in a mask. The mask is produced by Mr. Foley. One patient remarks about the mask, "I think it's great. It looks as if it were done by a person who really knows how to draw." Miss Callahan responds to the wish-fulfilling quality, "It sounds as if you mean it holds together and is unified." She picks up the group's (self's) wish to find life in Mr. Foley's face (the object). Although Mr. Foley lives among them, he is not truly one of them. They seek his form of adaptation to a vanishing self. Mr. Foley declares, "Help, I'm a rock." Mr. Novick dons his own mask in the role of flatterer, seeking to overshadow Mr. Foley. He comments that Miss Richards' and another young girl's drawings are "colorful and beautiful," while Mr. Foley's

Sequence VII: Group Regression. Stage 2: Statement. "JUNGLE," May 4, 1967, Mural #38.

is not. Irritated, Mr. Foley draws a "flowerlike fiendish thing," possibly alluding to his ambivalent attraction to these girls. A river of alligators and a man-eating plant depict the danger of the group devouring itself.

In "Fairyland" (#39) on May 11, the patients indicate their need to retreat from the destructive tendencies in each other. There is an immediate search for a protective mother as Mr. Foley enters, having just had a telephone conversation with his mother. His explosive mood conjures up the vision of his stony African mask of the previous week's mural. But before he can adjust his countenance, the sarcastic tone of Mr. Novick's invitation to join his group moves Mr. Foley to turn from this provocation to his aggressive impulses. He leaves the room. This act causes the group to react by fragmentation in the form of various distortions of space and time. Mr. Perlin, in a gesture typical for him, attempts to flee into space with Mr. Foley by suggesting Paris; or to flee to the past with Mr. Novick by suggesting a replay of the latter's scenario "French Revolution." Finally, Mr. Perlin completes his defense by suggesting "Fantasyland" with protective "fairy godmothers." Mr. Novick takes the suggestion further as he forces Mr. Perlin, his roommate, to submit "Fairyland." To emphasize his point Mr. Novick suggests that it could be "a reality theme." Miss Allen and Miss Meyers protectively intervene, stating that, "Fantasy is better than reality."

This statement seems to raise the curtain on the cardboard stage upon which magical images of the past will emerge. Miss Allen uses her pastel as a "Fairy Godmother's" wand, recalling the Cinderella story. Mr. Novick counterposes sinister cartoon images among the more reassuring visions of "once-upon-a-time." After he puts dandruff in Mr. Perlin's rendition of "Rapunzel's hair," Mr. Ronan is moved to draw a witch. The young girls in the group attempt to recoup the friendly image with

Sequence VII: Group Regression. Stage 3: Defense. "FAIRYLAND," May 11, 1967, Mural #39.

"Casper, the Friendly Ghost," and a smiling witch. Mr.
Perlin becomes increasingly disoriented, visibly paling
upon finding Miss Hecht sitting in his seat. Miss Allen
intervenes once again by calling for "Peter Pan." The
group of girls immediately breaks into an anxious chorus
of children's songs, which can not quite drown out Mr.
Perlin's entreaties. There is one last flutter of hope in
"Tinkerbell's" fairy wings. But Mr. Perlin, beyond personal hope, departs. Mr. Novick draws the curtain on the
cardboard stage by obliterating all available space. Miss
Allen says, "Like all comic books, it ends with 'continued
next week.' "

In this mural session, a defensive withdrawal from
reality proceeds through regression into the magical images of children. The defensive plunge, irreversible now,
gathers momentum, carrying the group closer to the
brink of self-annihilation on the one hand, and rebirth on
the other.

The mural of May 18th is called "Transylvania (#40).
In it, a monstrous being is brought to life. Excited sexual
and aggressive feelings are exposed by the group. Miss
Allen is quite excited. After she suggests Transylvania,
she says, "Let's do a little for the outside and a lot for the
inside." She also had suggested the theme "June is Bust-
ing Out All Over." This was in reference to her proposed
discharge in June. She looks forward to great freedom
and license to act out her impulses upon discharge. Ea-
gerly, she draws lightning and a body in front of the door
and a coffin with a lid. At this point she jokes about Dr.
Lukens, her therapist. Then she draws Frankenstein on a
table. Outside she depicts the black River Styx, a full
moon, and a mad scientist. Apparently, she enjoys the
idea of the therapist's power to liberate unknown impulses in her. She entertains the idea of killing him so
that these impulses might have free reign. Leaving the
hospital would be like killing the forces of restraint. Mr.

Sequence VII: Group Regression. Stage 3: Defense, continued. "TRANSYLVANIA," May 18, 1967, Mural #40.

Ronan draws the road leading to the door and a window with an electric machine visible inside of it. Then he draws a body on an operating table with an iron maiden in a mini-skirt, standing by her victim in the victim's blood. This is followed by a box with a visible leg and a detached head, and finally, a mad scientist touching the intestines of a monster. He animates the latter image by having a ghost say, "You better change that bedpan." Possibly Mr. Ronan represents Miss Allen as the iron maiden. At this time, Miss Allen has taken over some of the mothering function in the group. Mr. Ronan's drawing is full of terror and carnage. There is none of the playful distancing elements that occur in Miss Allen's productions. At about this time, on the ward, Mr. Ronan tells the nurse of his plan to electrocute himself with an electric plug while standing in his shower.

Throughout the preceding two murals, there have been repeated references to beings coming to life and to themes of rebirth and transformation. These themes reach the quintessence of their unconscious expression in the oceanic "Dreams" (#41) mural of May 25th. A suckling baby is portrayed in a scene replete with breast-balloons, sleeping pills and baby bottles.

Miss Allen draws a sailboat on a lake, surrounded by skyscrapers, and an airplane above the lake with a sickle-like projection from its propeller. Then she draws a volcano. At first this seems to present a picture of serenity menaced by the eruption of anger. However, if the analysis is continued in light of the theme of birth, Miss Allen's history becomes pertinent. She suffered a therapeutic abortion just prior to her admission to the ward. The dream scene which she has drawn is beautifully suited to represent her experience of the abortion. Then the boat on a lake becomes the foetus in its placental waters. The surrounding skyscrapers are the huge-seeming doctors who preside over the launching of the sailboat. The hover-

Stage VII: Group Regression. Stage 4: Unconscious. "DREAMS," May 25, 1967, Mural #41.

ing airplane with its sicklelike projection is the aborting instrument with its attached fear. Finally the volcano vents forth the fiery eruption of its contents.

Mr. Ronan draws a sleeping person, two sleeping pills, a heart and a purple sphinx. Everyone agrees that it is his own head which is portrayed on the sphinx's body. The themes of death in sleep, the death of feelings, and two beings in a single heart are readily perceived. The separation of head from body is a way of renouncing the feeling aspect of himself as well as demonstrating his lack of body unity. Comparing Miss Allen's use of symbolism with Mr. Ronan's reveals that the latter expresses the wish directly while the former uses the symbolism as disguise.

The next mural, called "L.S.D.," (#42) [1] is constructed during a period of covert marijuana smoking on the ward. Miss Allen, who is preparing for her departure from the ward, leads the group in portraying an excited gratification of all wishes. The element of acting out is added to the suggested resolution of rebirth. The patients want to act out new freedoms as new people.

The absence of Mr. Foley, one of the advocates of taking L.S.D., stimulates the theme of the mural. Miss Allen takes a leading role in its unfolding. Both Miss Allen and Mr. Foley are flower children in the sense that they have placed themselves in the frequent embrace of psychedelic drugs. There is an air of excitement as Miss Allen prepares to remove herself from the controls of the ward. She suggests "Crazy Animals" or "Animals and Flowers" for the theme. Undoubtedly, Mr. Foley is the prime example of a crazy animal and Miss Allen is the prime example of a flower. Another patient suggests a depiction of Miss Allen in the middle of crazy things as the theme. The patients are looking for life and excitement in the

[1] June 1, 1967. This mural is no longer available and this could not be reproduced here.

visual stimulation of some maternal image. Miss Allen draws a pipe with hashish smoke drifting upward. She follows this with flashing lights and multicolored flowers. Then she draws a face emerging from another patient's picture. She draws a wingless bee next to a flower, to which she then attaches huge wings. Finally, she contributes the face of someone high on L.S.D. Her productions indicate that, given the pretext of drugs, she would like to have sex with the big "B," the initial standing for Mr. Foley's first name. Mr. Ronan uses the theme of L.S.D. to allow himself even greater freedom in expressing his regressed images. He draws a coffinlike box containing an underwater eye which is plugged into an outlet. Then he draws a large mouth with a door in one of the teeth. In adding the rest of the face, he includes a moustache. Projecting from the eye of the face there is a mouth and from that mouth there projects another eye. Mr. Ronan is incorporating his moustachioed Dr. Lukens through a visual/oral mode. Mr. Ronan emulates his doctor's gestures and his doctor's intellectual manner. Once again he alludes to death and to the fluidity of his body concept. Certainly the death which he experiences is one of loss of feelings as well as loss of body integration.

The movement toward resolution of this sequence is impeded as those figures which have come to represent the desired maternal image are about to disappear. Miss Allen will be discharged and Miss Salvatore, the nurse, will leave the ward at the end of June. The group attempts to fix the image of the maternal face in order to avoid loss.

"Funny Faces" (#43) of June 7th portrays the commingling of mother and self in the image of a face. Miss Allen does not attend and Miss Selig, the most flagrantly psychotic patient, chooses the theme. The group draws peculiar, disorganized, disembodied faces. The epitome of this session occurs when Miss Richards draws a headless figure holding a balloon, upon which a face has been painted. The group laughs.

Mr. Ronan draws a white, ghostly face with a wide mouth and huge teeth. Then he draws a door with a face peering around it. Next he draws a face with a mirror reflection. The reflection is saying, "Don't you know it's not polite to stare?" He comments that Miss Allen is not present and at the end of the mural session he says that the door should be locked so that people don't wander out during the session. This apparent reference to reality concerns his desire to keep the maternal image of Miss Allen from leaving him. Once again, the visual and oral mode is employed to produce an incorporation. He cannot yet identify with his own image. He sees the face in the mirror as a kind of macabre enemy. His fluid face creates itself out of the swirling images of his senses.

The mural of June 14th, called "Beatles Album" (#44),[2] brings the group back toward its present reality. The sound of the Beatles is heard incessantly. This mural refers directly to episodes of marihuana smoking on the ward. The resolution finally portrayed involves abrogation of any real mother, and absorption into a maternal image.

When Miss Allen leaves the ward, she presents a gift of pot to several patients. Her contributions to this mural are a defiant reference to being stoned: tangerine trees, a stone-type kite and strawberry fields, all songs by the Beatles with direct reference to drug intake. She, too, must leave a mother behind and she resents, in the end, the freedom that she is attaining.

Mr. Novick's statement about the mural applies to the group: "It looks irresponsible. It had excitement in the beginning and then it cooled down." Another patient says, "A lot of adults aren't here." A third responds,

---

[2] The Beatles were a famous rock musical group who portrayed a search for the resolution of aggression through the beauty inherent in regressive self-expression.

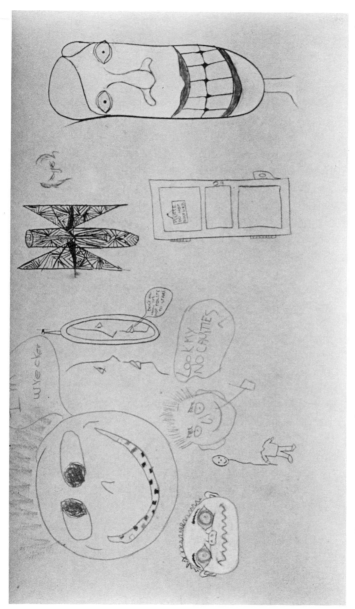

Sequence VII: Group Regression. Stage 5: Recombination. "FUNNY FACES," June 7, 1970, Mural # 43.

"How can you have fun when these people are breathing down your neck?"

Sequence VIII: Group Disintegration (6/21/67–8/2/67)

The final six weeks of the year's chronicle begins with the transfer of a confused cardiac patient from medicine. She dies a few days later. Subsequently, a young woman with self-inflicted, severe burns, is admitted for skin grafting and psychotherapy. Mrs. Reilly, a mature nurse, is allowed entry into her autistic world only with extreme caution.

Another schizophrenic youth is transferred from a State Hospital. He constantly threatens repugnant self-mutilation and is under round-the-clock observation. He repels and frightens most of the nursing staff.

A series of acts involving property destruction begins when a newly admitted patient breaks open a ward door and elopes. As if to celebrate, a large group of patients refuses to go to bed for one hour after curfew. There are no restrictive measures taken in reaction to this small rebellion. It seems that the therapists are rebelling as well, for often when on call they cannot be located. They are delinquent in renewing and even signing their orders.

Mr. Foley comes back in mid July, appearing penitent and humbled. He had been using psychedelic drugs during the last month and constantly talks about them. He no longer conceals his affection for Miss Jacobs and they are frequently found in each other's arms. As a result of numerous pressures, e.g., Miss Jacobs' consent "to go to bed with him," and another male patient's "declaration of love," Mr. Foley, that afternoon, with his own hands, breaks the 16 windows that line the nursing station and the dining-living room. He is not restrained.

Miss Salvatore's departure and the advent of vacations signal the finale to the year's chronicle. The staff group disbands itself in anticipation of the relief from the pres-

Sequence VII: Group Regression. Stage 6: Resolution "BEATLES ALBUM" June 14, 1967, Mural #44.

sures of 12-N. The patients become a sad band of nomads, searching for shelter in the arid reaches of the
ward, and finding only the institution's structure as a
support.

A new sequence begins once again with a depiction of
reality as realized in "The Many Faces of Miss Allen"
(#45). An attempt to hold on to Miss Allen, who has
been discharged, is made by the group through a recreation of her image. The patients feel angry because she
encouraged them to act out, only to leave them holding
the bag (pot). With reality in focus, the group is beginning to face a new period in which it must survive on its
own, i.e., without the protection of a mother-image.

Mr. Ronan suggests the theme of the mural. Other
suggestions were "Flower Power" and "False Loves," also
in reference to Miss Allen. Mr. Ronan draws a large bugle with notes emanating from it. Miss Allen had obtained a job as a camp counsellor with the provision that
she play reveille each morning. Then he depicts Miss
Allen saying, "How dare you be in my way," to a brick
wall. Another blurb depicts her saying, "Jesus Christ, will
you give me my bugle and go away." He then draws an
image of a woman's lips on money, alleging that Miss
Allen's sweet lips may be bought. In this mural, Mr.
Ronan expresses the group's anger toward Miss Allen.
He represents her as using anything or anyone to get her
way. In expressing anger, his imagery appears less psychotic.

On June 28, 1967, the members of the group enter the
room almost en masse. It is their usual habit to arrive
intermittently, one by one and two by two. On this occasion, however, they can hardly wait for the door to open.
At other times when they arrived in this manner, it was
learned that they had discussed and planned the mural
over lunch. This time there had been no prior discussion
or planning but rather a spontaneous desire to express a

commonly felt need. They herded themselves into the room and sat for a moment in silent contemplation of the drab gray panel in front of them. Miss Siegel is the first to speak. "Let's choose," she says impatiently as she stares straight ahead at the panel. Mr. Ronan's response is immediate. "Flower Power," is the first theme suggestion. The ideas which follow come in a steady barrage. Mr. Novick seeks escape by a "Trip on Morning Glory Seeds." Mrs. Foster also feels the urge to get away with "People on Vacation." An important substitution is about to take place in the leadership as Dr. Evans, a proponent of the more permissive treatment approach, prepares to take over while Dr. Schwartz vacations. Dr. Evans' patients, Miss Siegel, Miss Jacobs, and Mrs. Foster have become more active in the mural sessions.

Miss Siegel follows Mrs. Foster with "a mural of us drawing a mural." This is a theme she had suggested at other mural sessions. Mrs. Foster again prefers "a theme with more leeway." Miss Siegel, responds to Mrs. Foster, "How about a swimming pool?" Mrs. Weil calls for "a rainy day." "A funny thing happened on the way to the hospital," is Mr. Ronan's latest idea. One of the newer patients on the ward, Mr. Davidson, looks confused as he asks, "What is this all about?" Misses Siegel, Richards and Jacobs take turns explaining the mural's purpose. He thanks them and the theme suggestions continue to pour forth. Miss Jacobs: "Barefoot in the hospital"; Mr. Novick: "The bust in the hospital"; Mr. Ronan: "The Weinberg Affair"; Mrs. Foster: "Bust." Miss Siegel, clinging to Mrs. Foster, follows her for the third straight time, "When you get caught," she yells.

The theme suggestions have been fluctuating between the return to a reality scene as in the case of "a mural of us drawing a mural," and movement toward the unconscious, suggested by themes such as the "swimming pool" or the drug-inspired "trip on morning glory seeds."

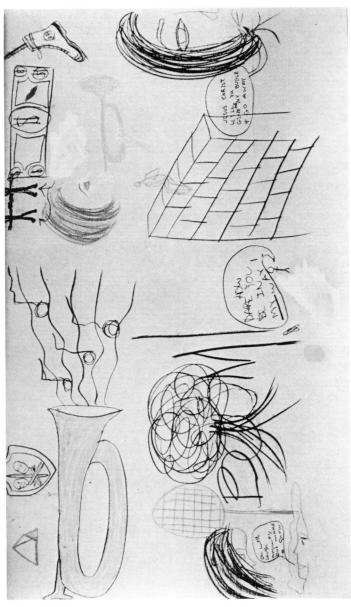

Sequence VIII: Group Disintegration. Stages 1 & 2: Reality & Statement. "THE MANY FACES OF MISS ALLEN" June 21, 1967, Mural #45.

At this point, the hurried exit from the room by a new patient, Mrs. Bernstein, brings the deluge to an end. Gradually, the movement away from reality is gathering force. The group turns momentarily from its concern about a mural theme to talk sorrowfully about her leaving. They tell each other how sorry they are for "poor old Mrs. Bernstein," whereupon they quickly return to their brainstorming task. Their efforts to vote on what they have are largely unsuccessful. Then somebody announces, "We need a new idea." After a brief moment of silence, Mr. Novick says, in a voice that gives the word its definition, "Anxiety" (#46). The group's vociferous response signaled the end of the search. Cries of, "Flip out, freak out, let's get it on," are the viva voce ratification of Mr. Novick's solicitous suggestion.

In other murals of defense, the patients frequently used a particular theme to avoid direct manifestations of anxiety. They would for example, escape to "a country place," or even to some imagined haven of childhood like, "Big rock candy mountain." Here, however, the defensive maneuvers are insufficient to stem a flood tide of anxiety, which ultimately leads to massive regression and an abandonment of the group mind to the realm of the unconscious.

The anxiety is portrayed through faces, some of which are recognizable as group members, as in the case of Mr. Ronan, who rushes to the panel along with Mr. Novick and Miss Richards. Mr. Ronan, who is the first to draw, sketches a man's face which, according to the group, resembles himself. He angrily responds, "That's how I freak out." Others show how they freak out. Mr. Novick waves a red flag from the center of a spiral form. Miss Richards draws a cross-eyed face with a huge zig-zag mouth which, according to Mrs. Weil, is a likeness. More symbols of anxiety emerge as Mr. Novick adds a large devouring mouth reflecting his fear of being consumed. This evokes the comment, "Wow, that's a scream!" from Miss Siegel and a shudder of horror from Mrs. Weil. Miss Richards' arrow, shot from the center of a spiral, finds its mark. Mr. Novick, seeking to contain the symbolic upheaval within the framework of his own limitations for aggression, springs to the panel and frames the mural in red. Seeing this as his bid to harness and take control of the mural's aggressive elements, Miss Jacobs reacts with, "Flip-outs aren't controlled." She is quickly informed by Miss Siegel, "In here they are." Mr. Novick tries desperately to rule the action. By altering, and adding to the works of others, he attempts to make it all speak just for him. He is challenged by Mrs. Foster about touching the other patients' drawings and an uptight Mr. Ronan threatens to become even more so as Mr. Novick adds some tears to the face he drew. Mrs. Foster's challenge is reminiscent of the rules which had been agreed upon much earlier during the group's infancy when the inviolable nature of an individual's contribution was first formulated.

Mr. Novick's persistence brings a word of caution from the therapist, Mr. Blackman, and a reminder of the need for permission to alter another's work. In response, Mr. Novick apologizes and proceeds to wipe away his tears from Mr. Ronan's face. Mr. Blackman urges other group members to draw. Mr. Ronan, feeling the pressure of his unexpressed anger weighing him down, draws an anvil on the stomach of a prone figure. Mr. Novick's overwhelming fear of death tricks him into seeing a tombstone in the anvil's place. The other members of the group have become mere spectators, watching Mr. Novick and Mr. Ronan do their thing. They urge each other to participate, suggesting various objects to draw. This is further indica-

Sequence VIII: Group Disintegration. Stage 3: Defense. "ANXIETY," June 28, 1967, Mural #46.

tion that the group is losing its differentiated structure.

Miss Siegel adds a scribble and some color. Another new patient, who enters the room later after a session with her doctor, is asked to guess the theme of the mural. "Mr. Novick's anxiety attacks," is her instantaneous and astonishing reply. He immediately defends, insisting that the anxiety is "everyone's." Miss Richards is wrenched from her stillness. She rushes to the panel to claim her rightful share in the feeling. Her long drawn out "AAAAAHHH" is an underscore to Mr. Novick's protest. Miss Siegel claims her part by writing "SHIT." Then Mr. Novick in a final move to dominate the scene calls for an end to the mural by laying the theme and his fears to rest beneath a tombstone on which he writes "R.I.P. anxiety." Not content to let it end with a statement other than his own, Mr. Ronan punctuates the mural with a broken exclamation point, an expression of his brokenness and continuing need to be made whole. Seen another way, the broken exclamation point is Mr. Ronan's concrete pun on the "R.I.P." of Novick's tombstone. Here, all the cries of anguish die and serenity is found in the grave.

Miss Siegel finds Mr. Novick's grave "peaceful." Miss Richards makes the comment, "Love that grave." The patients' escape from primitive separation anxiety has led them to a death scene. Death becomes a way of portraying the unconscious as well as representing the disintegration of the group's structure, in the unfolding process of group schizophrenia.

Mr. Blackman encourages the group to comment on the mural. It is seen alternately as a "joke" and a serious expression of the patients' fears of abandonment by the staff or separation from the hospital's protective environment.

The next mural, "An Island" (#47), is a classical depiction of the topographic unconscious. A land/water division reflects the structural dilemma of how to get back to the mainland of reality, the world of other people. The mural portrays a variety of regressive attempts to handle object loss, and its attendant anger. One suggestion for the theme was, "The Many Faces of Miss Callahan." The aggressive process of splitting the object into its component images is a way of killing yet keeping the object, dehumanizing it like a snapshot. In that disparate images are closer to the senory origin of the object, they represent it more concretely.

"Civil War," "World War III," and "Being Discharged and Hit by a Truck" are other theme suggestions which reveal the wish to obliterate the self if the necessary object is gone. The order of contributions to this mural reveals the process of structural dislocation and destruction of the self.

The self is an island, isolated and deserted. It calls for help (message in a bottle). There is no answer. It tries to span the gap to the object (airplane, birds, boat, train, pulling the plug). It cannot. It regresses to magic omnipotence (a genie). It retreats into an inner core of strength, the hospital itself (a fortress is built on the island). Now the self is safe, reunited in the object. The whole area of the mural is declared under the jurisdiction of L.B.J., who is paradoxically declaring himself unavailable at this time.

The entire mural, suggesting a process of group schizophrenia, fits Mr. Ronan's mode of existence. It was he who proposed the "Civil War" theme. After the island concept was accepted, his first contribution was a head with two faces attached to a body. Then when the group tried to bridge the gap to the mainland of the object, Mr. Ronan contributed a drain with a plug to empty the water. Another patient drew a cigarette in one of the two mouths. Mr. Ronan responded verbally, saying, "This is a

Sequence VIII: Group Disintegration. Stage 4: Unconscious. "AN ISLAND," July 6, 1967, Mural # 47.

pretty empty island." Then he drew a long-stemmed rose in a goblet, and railroad tracks. His last contribution was a flag announcing, "L.B.J. was here," "This is now under jurisdiction of Texas."

The suggestion of "Civil War" in addition to its historical reference reflects the war within his own inner states. The two-faced head, one of his favorite contributions, reveals the schizophrenic split between thought and feeling, and within the self, between subjective images and mirror-type images, which so often seem to represent him. His answer to the group's dilemma of how to reestablish contact with the protective environment is contained in his next contribution of pulling the plug and letting the separating waters drain out. Mr. Ronan's previous references to plugs and bathrooms have revealed suicidal wishes. Presumably, it is his own vital fluids that he wishes to disperse so that he can become the ghost figure that he depicts so often. Bathroom imagery often refers to a child's fears that he will disappear in much the same manner as bath and toilet water or feces. Now, when someone places a cigarette in the mouth of the self he has drawn, he declares that it is nevertheless an empty island. It must be so because his subjective self has been abandoned. Now he fashions a long-stemmed rose in a goblet. This recasts the imagery of the cigarette in the mouth, and now it is he in the mouth of his mother, being swallowed up to merge with her image. A set of railroad tracks represents his movement inward. Finally, he draws the curiously inscribed flag. If L.B.J. represents the powerful external therapist/mother which has been lost or will be lost at vacation time, then the regression allows the more primitive L.B.J. mother/therapist to reign in the mind. It is now the lost object's image which has jurisdiction in the mind through a process of swallowing the self. Mr. Ronan always loved the book *Gone with the Wind*. He would return again and again to the lost plantation in the South where the heroine must call it a new day alone. Mr. Ronan's self, having lost the Civil War, returns to a primitive, undifferentiated state. During Dr. Lukens' vacation, Mr. Ronan will decide to cut his food intake drastically. He says that he must become thin in order to achieve a state of perfection. In his discussions of the state of perfection, Mr. Ronan says that he must be delicate, graceful, a perfect "princess." To him, perfection implies that his own self would disappear entirely, being replaced by an ideal largely composed of early maternal imagery.

On July 12, just prior to Dr. Lukens' departure, "Old Movies" (#48) is constructed. The information available about this mural is scant, probably because of the general attitude of withdrawal at the time. Mr. Ronan depicts "Strange Interlude" by Eugene O'Neill. The title refers to the period of his therapist's absence. O'Neill's characters wear masks. The connection with the preceding material is obvious. It was Mr. Ronan who suggested the theme of "Old Movies," indicating a straightforward wish to substitute past images for the present.

The mural of July 19, entitled "Brain Damage," portrays the destruction of doctors and a mental patient. Mr. Ronan draws a razor blade with eyeballs and a clock reading two o'clock. This is nearly a suicidal threat, in the nature of a reference to the time of his proposed demise. The brain, itself, becomes the damaged haven of the group.

In this mural, "Mythology in General" (#50), the images of fusion reach back beyond the pale of the ward. Inarticulate, disheartened, the staff cannot produce viable notes. It is as if not even the most primitive theme can still represent the life of the group.

In the very last mural, coinciding with a large exodus of staff for vacations, the theme becomes Miss Callahan leaving, a condensation of all the losses that occur. There

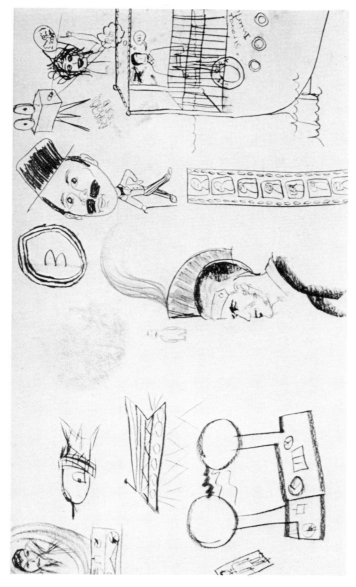

Sequence VIII: Group Disintegration. Stage 5: Recombination. "OLD MOVIES," July 12, 1967, Mural #48.

Sequence VIII: Group Disintegration. Stage 5: Recombination, continued. "BRAIN DAMAGE," July 19, 1967, Mural #49.

Sequence VIII: Group Disintegration. Stage 5: Recombination, continued. "MYTHOLOGY IN GENERAL," July 26, 1967, Mural #50.

Stage VIII: Group Disintegration. Stage 6: Resolution. "LEAVING," August 2, 1967, Mural #51.

is a lengthy pause; the cardboard face of the mural is without form. The therapist says, "The cardboard is blank." A patient responds, "That's the mural; everyone is gone." A stick figure is drawn followed by the face of Miss Callahan and her male assistant who is also leaving. Finally an airplane is added, inscribed with the names of Miss Callahan and her assistant, and carrying an antenna for communication. Mr. Novick draws Superman. Mr. Ronan comments that Miss Callahan and her assistant gave life to the group . . . their life. Then lightning hits the airplane. As an epilogue, Mr. Ronan asks Mr. Novick, "Why Superman?"

His reply: "It gives life to the mural."

5

STRUCTURE FORMATION

Group Development

THE FOREGOING MURAL sequences may be used as a tool for the analysis of the group's development as each mural emerges from the ongoing experience of the group. In this analysis the emphasis will *not* be on those aspects of the group which relate to its successive periods of drive organization such as the oral, anal, phallic; or dependency, power and intimacy. The aggressive derivatives of these phases are rather to be viewed in the context of their interaction with the mental representations of the milieu. Successive processes of identification lead to a hierarchical structural organization of the group's ego. The confluence of forces in each mural session is such that each member can identify with the task as if it were a task which could be encompassed by a single individual. At any moment each group member experiences the group in terms of his own present structural organization.

Aggression and Group Structure

Reconstructing the history of the ward shows that the single most important element affecting the ward's life is the manner in which aggression is to be handled. This in

turn depends on the developmental level of the drive derivative and the group's relation to its leader figure. Once
a group structure has been developed, it provides the
context for any change in the manner in which the group
handles its aggressive conflicts. The sequential development of the group recapitulates the structural development of an individual. The first sequence is concerned
with the question of trust; i.e., the patients' trust that they
will not destroy one another. The first group structure
grows out of this need. This question is equally valid for
the staff. In that a nucleus of the staff had worked together
before the ward's opening, sufficient time had passed for
the establishment of two factions: "liberal" and "conservative." As the mural "A Home" (#6) shows, a viable
group must provide more than one point of view about
issues. Aggressive forces structure the group into factions. The two factions which arise can be identified by
their manner of responding to hostility. The "conservatives" use their own aggression to squelch the open
expression of hostility in others, while the "liberals,"
fearful of their own aggression, endorse its expression by
others. When Dr. Isaacson, the conservative Director,
wants to clamp down on open expression, he chooses
Miss Marsh, the nurses' proponent of liberalism, as his
target. When Dr. Evans, liberal Admissions Chief, wants
to "open things up more" on the ward, he opposes Miss
Conrad, the conservative Head Nurse. He argues that she
should stop suppressing the patients. This homeostatic
system using aggression as a basis for group structural
cleavage bears certain similarities with the stage of symbiotic relationship that develops between a mother and
child. Primary identifications of like with like determine
who fits on which side, and the primary defense of splitting
maintains the staff's cleavage into subject (vehicle of
aggression) and object (target of aggression).

In the second sequence the group's polar structure is

threatened by new patients and the staff's polarity is threatened by the tendency for each individual to strike off on his own. This problem is eventually solved by allowing subgroup formation to point the way to individuation and cooperation. The staff members differentiate in their roles as individuals. This differentiation occurs under pressure of a fear of criticism. Basically, the staff fears to incur the displeasure of Dr. Isaacson and Miss Conrad. Translated to the individual level, staff members fear infringing on each other's zones of activity. Concomitantly, in the mural group there is a great deal of concern about whether one patient may alter in any way the contribution of another patient. This trend can be followed through the sequence to its resolution of respect for one another's contribution.

When nurses come in to observe the mural they are welcomed as potential helpers by the activities staff. However, Miss Conrad, fearing nurses will be used as adjuncts and taken away from their own responsibilities, blocks such activities. Activities personnel are reluctant to perform such "nursing" functions as rousing patients from sleep even if, as a result, patients miss the beginning of an activity. Thus, a kind of professional guarding and differentiation of roles arises in response to intrastaff hostility. From the point of view of symbiotic ego structure, the group is threatened by orally derived envy and hostility as "outsiders" begin to intrude. The hostility which is felt with regard to "outsiders" is restricted in its expression by the group's conservative leaders. This measure facilitates the formation of a separation-individuation stage of development as an available means of channeling the aggressive drives. Even the liberal Mr. Blackman is sometimes experienced as a conservative leader in the mural setting, since he conveys the ground rules.

In the third sequence the parallel development between

staff and patient groups continues to be manifest. As Dr. Isaacson must limit his presence on the ward, the question becomes how to maintain the integrity of the group in the absence of his immediate authority. Other losses, such as Miss Cooper's discharge, must be overcome by the patient group. At first the action follows what has been proposed in the analysis of stages. The patients defensively withdraw and some actually "elope." Irritated and disillusioned staff members also withdraw. The realization of their own lack of omnipotence as the patients withdraw contributes to the staff's withdrawal. The members of staff become angry with Dr. Isaacson for what they consider his sporadic leadership. As troubles multiply the anger between conservatives and liberals increases. Finally, Dr. Isaacson issues an edict proclaiming the conservative faction in control but in effect directing his authority through Dr. Schwartz, the part-time Assistant Director. In response the group internalizes the Director's values by suppressing hostility and by proceeding to commiserate and work with one another. As with the patients, members of staff begin to develop a sense of empathy for one another. In terms of the group's "ego" development, an "identification with the aggressor" employed by the different members of the group allows the recognition of a common experience. The newly acquired images can be used as an element in the synthesis of group structure. The group develops a reactive posture toward its sadistic strivings such that each person is equally responsible for suppressing hostility in any group member, including himself. The representation of an "adult" object functions to focus controlling aggression on the more infantile self. This mechanism for compromising between the inner anal aggressive derivatives and the aggression experienced as emanating from the outside, becomes the structuring force for the group. Autonomy results from this mechanism.

In the fourth sequence, the staff cannot maintain its spirit of cooperation and the inculcation of the director's values. As the stimuli of the work load increase, new problems, new desires, new frustrations, and new aggressions are in the offing. Dr. Schwartz is not yet fully invested with the mantle of leadership. Dr. Augress, Dr. Isaacson's right-hand fellow, is the first scapegoat. Nursing complains about the lack of direction from doctors. Frustrated oedipal strivings lead to attitudes of jealousy displaced to various subgroups and individuals.

When Mr. Novick is admitted and assigned by Dr. Evans to Dr. Augress, he becomes a focus for both the staff and the patients. He is able to take over the murals without so much as a murmur of protest from the other patients. As the sequence evolves it becomes clear that by abrogating to Mr. Novick the patients create a future scapegoat. At this time, Dr. Schwartz, a liberal, is resented for his affiliation with Miss Conrad, a conservative. Oedipal feelings of jealousy mar the previous resolutions. In his capacity of directing administrative ward conferences, Dr. Schwartz carefully tries to promote logical rules for conduct among the staff and for the patients. In terms of the ward's "ego" development, a father figure has been internalized (Dr. Isaacson), reprojected (Dr. Schwartz), and displaced onto other figures (Mr. Novick, Dr. Augress). Dr. Schwartz even helps to promote a kind of moral legislation of authority (superego). By turning its hostility toward a substitute figure, the group manages to protect the internalized image of authority, while developing a representational focus of authority. In the first six months of its life the ward has developed "ego" structures in successive stages by its creative approach to handling aggression. This development has depended on the consistent tone of control and suppression which emanates from Dr. Isaacson and from the group's need for a Dr. Isaacson.

CHART 4

FATE OF THE GROUP SELF AND OBJECT REPRESENTATIONS IN THE DISINTEGRATIVE PHASE OF THE MURAL

DATE	TITLE	CREATIVE STAGE	GROUP STRUCTURE AS RELATIONSHIP BETWEEN SELF AND OBJECT
Sequence V:			
2/2/67	Inferno	Statement	Object (Father) threatens to engulf (burn in hell) self (group)
2/9/67	Winter Scene	Defensive	Object is dehumanized (symbolized as a snowman)
2/16/67	Big Rock Candy Mt.	Defensive	Self wishes to eat object (gingerbread man)
2/23/67	Mobiles	Defensive	Self is alone, object gone
3/2/67	Beautiful Underwater Scene	Unconscious	Self and object attempt to incorporate and kill each other
3/9/67	Fence	Unconscious/ Recombination	Self kills object
3/16/67	French Revolution	Recombination	Self kills object
3/23/67	Operating Room	Resolution	Self kills object and becomes object
Sequence VI:			
3/30/67	Zoo	Reality/ Statement	Self functions smoothly with internalized object
4/6/67	End of the World	Statement/ Defense	Self disintegrates, object is reprojected
4/13/67	Emotions	Unconscious	Self loses bodily representation
4/20/67	Doctors & Patients	Resolution	Self and object both lose body continuity

DATE	TITLE	CREATIVE STAGE	GROUP STRUCTURE AS RELATIONSHIP BETWEEN SELF AND OBJECT
Sequence VII:			
4/22/67	Abstract	Reality	Self has no representational outward existence
5/4/67	Jungle	Statement	Self seeks representation in a mask
5/11/67	Fairyland	Defensive	Self seeks life in projected maternal images (good & bad)
5/18/67	Transylvania	Defensive/ Unconscious	Self seeks life in object (bad mother) through being devoured
5/25/67	Dreams	Unconscious/ Recombination	Self seeks life in object (good mother) through devouring (sucking)
6/1/67	LSD	Recombination/ Resolution	Self is excited by object's face (maternal image)
6/7/67	Funny Faces	Resolution	Self and object united in mother's face (part object)
6/14/67	Beatles Album	Resolution/ Reality	Self disappears in object
Sequence VIII:			
6/21/67	The Many Faces of Miss Allen	Reality/ Statement	Object (maternal face) is split and destroyed
6/28/67	Anxiety	Defensive	Object is split and destroyed (faces)
7/6/67	An Island	Unconscious	Object and self both are gone—replaced by unity
7/12/67	Old Movies	Recombination	A false self/object unity
7/19/67	Brain Damage	Recombination/ Resolution	No self or object
7/26/67	Mythology in General	Resolution	Life is sought in self-object unity (power)
8/2/67	Leaving	Resolution/ Reality	Life is sought in (uterus?)

Group Self

As the group's life develops it becomes increasingly complex. Even new patients cannot disrupt the tone of continuing movement. At this point the group seems to have created a kind of organism with a life of its own. In the mural group the choice of theme for construction and subsequent discussion all tend to unify the group around a common focus. In order to deal with the increasing complexity in the group it will be assumed that the group has reached a stage of integration where it is meaningful to speak of its having a self and object. Indeed, this assumption seems implicit in every group member. In the last four sequences this assumption is essential to understanding what happens.

The loss of authority figures enhances a regression of the group self in the latter six months. During the fifth sequence Miss Conrad becomes ill and the staff's rebellious oedipal feelings yield progressively to a sense of guilt. Chart 4 illustrates the movement during the sequence. Mr. Novick, the group's appointed leader, attempts to maintain control over the group as he sadistically opposes them. Gradually the group withdraws from him by acting as if he does not exist in reality. Finally, in the "Beautiful Underwater Scene" (#29) of the unconscious, the aggression of the group and Mr. Novick's aggression do battle. As the resolution of this period approaches in "Fence" (#30) and "French Revolution" (#31) the group repeatedly kills its tormentor, that is, Mr. Novick. Unable to withstand the group's infernal pressure, Mr. Novick joins them and becomes the chief proponent of the group's outward-directed sadism. However, the group now finds itself in the position of having no leader, not even the one appointed as scapegoat. In the final mural of this sequence, "Operating Room" (#32), Dr. Lukens becomes the object of the group's sadism and intense guilt produces a movement to "save" Dr.

Lukens. The group finally concludes that it is not Dr. Lukens who has been killed but rather the "sick me."

In "Operating Room" (#32) ritual murder is finally completed, but the essence or spirit of the dead man is liberated. This indicates the availability of the dead man's spirit to enter into the body of the patient, a suitable symbol for identification. Consideration of the protocol and of the entire sequence yields an insight into the process of oedipal identification. The group and the staff are coping with a loss of the authority figure through a process of identification. First, this means turning a passive loss into an active one by finding a scapegoat. Then it means coping with the liberated aggression and with the enormous sadistic gratification of the killing. The "bad" or cruel aspects of the object are the first to be internalized as they are identified with the group's (self's) own hostility. This means that the feeling of aggression is equated with the object. In the unconscious, the object and the self are fused on the basis of their common "badness," i.e., aggressive cathexis. But then the self becomes too "bad" or aggressive to tolerate. Ensuing guilt serves to bind the aggression, to neutralize it and to relieve the self of its unacceptable structural component of badness. Now the object, having been purified, can be identified with, in its ideal aspect. The object is preserved as an aspect of an acceptable self.

The oral-incorporative aspects of this identification must also be considered. The sequence, which began as the group itself was engulfed, ends with a reversal of this process in which the object is engulfed or swallowed. The oral aspect proceeds from roasting the group, to the "Big Rock Candy Mountain" (#27) with its central gingerbread man, to the voracious fishes of the mural of the unconscious to the gingerbread house of the "Fence" (#30) mural. The carnage of the "French Revolution" (#31) and the "Operating Room" (#32) scene serve as preparation for a final totem feast.

From the oedipal point of view, the threatening mother and father are killed in fantasy and guilt forces an identification with them. The staff creates its own variation on the theme as Dr. Schwartz is regarded in a way similar to Mr. Novick. Although he is not treated this way directly, his patient, Mrs. Hecht, becomes the focus of the ward's concern. She is related to with anger, and only when she undergoes her own symbolic death by a failure to eat, does the staff mobilize itself to "save" her. Through saving her, Dr. Schwartz is in effect saved as well. In the end of this sequence each person can survive without a leader because his own aggression is partitioned off in the form of a "bad side" to his nature.

Despite internal transformation, the group is not capable of functioning without a clearly defined leader. Now it is also burdened with a sense of guilt, a mechanism which is ready to attack mental structure. In the sixth sequence, the group-self loses its intactness in the face of a threat. In the "Zoo" (#33) mural, which starts the sequence, a beautifully intact group still flourishes. The internalized object is thriving within the group's self. The group enjoys a totem banquet as it contemplates its future. Freud's analysis of *Totem and Taboo* is not only relevant, but capable of further expansion in light of the present group.

On "Totem and Taboo"

In 1913 Freud published a series of articles which made use of psychoanalytically derived insights to help explain some of the mysteries inherent in the complicated use of totems by many different societies. A totem is some object, usually an animal, which is endowed by a particular clan or group with extreme significance and power to influence all of the vital functions in individual and societal life. Freud noted that the kind of thinking, animistic, which characterized the regard for the totem object, was identical with the magical qualities with which young children endow their thoughts. Further he observed many similarities between thought magic and the unconscious fantasies which he had discovered underlying the structure of neurosis. The power of such thoughts are embodied by primitive societies in taboos. These were social regulations governing the conduct toward special individuals as well as toward totem animals. If taboos, such as the laws of exogamy, i.e., the necessity for keeping sexual relations directed out of the clan, were violated, then the power would be loosed on the offending individual. This could take the form of invasion by spirits or ghosts until the offending individual was destroyed.

Freud regarded the totemistic stage as a phase in the development of societies, to be superceded by religious and finally scientific phases as cultural maturity occurred. By integrating the various theses concerning the origin of totemic power, Freud concluded that it stemmed from the Oedipus complex. The taboo against intercourse with a maternal figure and the taboo against usurping the leader's power, central in the totem society, are the two essential elements in the Oedipus complex. Freud argued, with some anthropological merit, that a central series of events led to the structure of totem societies and that these events were equivalent to a fantasied oedipal triumph.

A primal horde of brother figures rally their forces to defeat and kill the feared and powerful primal father figure. In a spirit of great celebration, they partake in a communal meal of the fallen figure's flesh. His substance imparts his power to them, but a deep sense of guilt tempers the triumph. At first the totem animal became the ritual replacement of the father figure; when the fantasy is reenacted with this substitute, it is called the "totem feast." The sense of guilt produces a taboo against any further manifestation of this primal fantasy and the totem animal is elaborated to embody the prohibitions as well as the power of the original father figure, thus serving as the basis for the rules of the society.

In his conclusion Freud admits that his theories presuppose a kind of collective mind which is analogous to an individual mind. He wonders how such a primal deed can communicate itself to successive generations, retaining its full force and unconscious content.

Those focal questions can better be approached if Freud's theoretical context of that particular time is noted. His instinct theory still considered as the basic dichotomy, the conflict between the sexual and the self-preservative drives. Although he recognizes in the concept of ambivalence that hostility to the father figure is focal, he had not yet elaborated his instinct theory to the position where sexual and aggressive drives represent the basic instinctual dichotomy. He also had not developed a structural theory, so that, for instance, he would view spirits or ghosts purely as projections of instinct (sexual). When he speaks about fear of the dead, although he emphasizes the preexisting ambivalence to the dead figure, he had not yet concluded as he did later in *Mourning and Melancholia* (1917) that an identification with the dead person is set up in the person's ego. In *Group Psychology and the Analysis of the Ego* Freud (1921) moves further toward explaining the common identifications with the father figure which underlie group unity, providing therewith some basis for a "collective mind." The structuralization of aggressive drive derivatives inherent in the Totem laws could not be stated explicitly in his theory.

The present study of group structure notes that a whole sequence corresponds in great detail to Freud's reconstruction of the totem society. Examination of this sequence, especially its culmination, is illuminating. First, as to the correspondence, Mr. Novick, the group leader in sequence four, is gradually dehumanized and forced to undergo a series of repetitive symbolic murders in sequence five. This has been well documented. Throughout the sequence Mr. Novick is alluded to more and more in terms of oral imagery. The major change in Mr. Novick's role is from an object that punishes the group to a subject who expresses and channels the group's sadistic thrust outward. As this structural change in the group occurs, the members find a new outlet for their sadism in the symbolic torture and murder of Dr. Lukens. His patients, Miss Allen, Mrs. Popidopolus and Mr. Phillips, have been most influential during the sequence. As the sequence ends, Dr. Lukens is dying on the operating table and there is a movement to save him. First he is transformed to Dr. X, whereupon the patients say that his spirit can live by entering into those who are still living. Finally it is concluded that the "bad me" has died, not Dr. Lukens. Thus a particular symbol of identification has been created which serves to bind the group's individual aggression with the form of incorporated object. The actual totem feast is symbolically but nevertheless clearly portrayed in the following "Zoo" (#33) mural.

Returning to the description of this zoo mural, the reader can make a number of observations. The relevance of this group experience to the totem feast is seen in the "Banquet" suggestion following the long process of "killing" Mr. Novick. The movement of theme suggestions goes to Last Supper, Sculpture Garden and finally to the Zoo. Perhaps most striking are the man-eating qualities of the animals. The man who is eaten and then identified with is first Mr. Novick, but then the various doctors. Each patient works toward developing his own symbolic animal guise. The connection between a totem animal and the father and incorporated leader substantiates Freud's observations about the relevance of this mechanism. One interesting divergence from Freud's supposition of a group mind is the female orientation of the current group. Freud presupposes a collection of brother figures who share the fallen leader's power. In the patient group there are also elements of feminine competition for the possession of the leader's identity.

During this mural session the timing of the movement from theme selection to mural production to discussion depends on the momentary ability of members to resolve their hostile and competitive feelings toward each other.

If a primal father figure disappears or is killed, then the group is faced not only with a competitive urge to usurp his power, but with the necessity for finding some means of controlling the hostility it harbors toward other members of the group. History reveals repeatedly that after a revolution there is bloodshed among the supporters of the revolution. Thus a function of the identification with the father leader through his totem presentation is to provide a structure whereby the resultant liberated hostility is bound. As Freud (1921) points out, the element of mutual identification with the existing leader is a way of making equals of the group members and resolving competitive strivings. Mr. Phillips personifies the ideal spirit of the fallen father as he presides as high priest over the totem procedings. Mr. Novick personifies the "evil" or exorcised spirit of the fallen father. Since neither can effectively maintain the role in reality, the internalization process is stimulated.

One basis of the totem function then is to preserve group structure by binding competitive individual hostility through a process of parallel identification. The animal form stands for an incorporating entity which is convenient for symbolizing orality and identity.

The group is also reassured of its continuing power

through the internal preservation of the leader. The totem animal comes to represent externally the process of identification which has occurred. In this way the group's external structure is modelled on the very process of identification. The celebration proclaiming a fusion with the idealized aspect of the incorporated body further verifies Freud's (1921) conclusion that such a mechanism is at work.

Note is taken that the Totem mural (i.e., "Zoo," #33) begins a new sequence, coming after the completion of the period of revolution. The timing indicates that the totem feast is related to the structure of the group as it is to exist in reality. The fact that it occurs during the disintegrative period of the group's existence is related generally to the lack of an available, i.e., physically present leader, so that replacement by a mental representation is facilitated. The danger of a real oedipal triumph is the liberation of hostility among those who are left without a reliable focus of strength. The mutual identification with the absent figure is mutually externalized in an animal form in the totem society, or at an abstract level is externalized as a moral principle of group conduct. Despite this mechanism, the group like a five-year-old is left powerless to cope with the real threat of a powerful intruder. The previous mechanisms of primary identification of subject and object, oral incorporation and introjection, anal identification with the aggressor, and internalization of the object representation into the self-representation, must all be employed to pierce the hierarchy of previous structural solutions in order to produce the present mechanism of symbolizing the abstract essence of the leader.

The next mural of this sequence is entitled "End of the World" (#34). Here, the group gives itself up to the ravages of guilt, the instrument of which is Mr. Foley. Mr. Phillips is gone and Mr. Novick will not attend. In the "Doctors and Patients" (#36) mural which ends the sequence bodies are portrayed with large holes and disembodied parts; phalluses and breasts are depicted. The patients feel that the staff is not protecting them and at this point, without other resources, they give in to disintegration. The rupture of their collective self-image liberates a diffuse aggression which is directed toward the image of doctors. Mr. Novick leads in a kind of cartoon attack on the image of doctors. Thus the resolution of this sequence is to permit a symbolic castration of the group's instrumental function, to the point where the group no longer has any real means of expressing its aggression.

In the seventh sequence the group finds itself essentially helpless as it has no longer any means of expressing its aggression. It turns regressively to mother figures and toward its more infantile past. The character of the murals is changing. They no longer have a connotative richness such that mural content refers to the group's relation to reality, but rather represent the more concrete and idiosyncratic expressions of a psychotic group. The first mural in Sequence VII is called "Abstract," or alternately "Body Insides." A reading of the description of this mural session reveals how much the group finds itself without a tangible means of physical integration. It is merely stating its reality dilemma. On the ward, Dr. Isaacson is still busy elsewhere and Miss Conrad is still sick. Miss Marsh is unable to administer the nursing staff and Dr. Schwartz is still not empowered. Although Mr. Foley has become somewhat more tranquil and will be discharged during this period, the aggressive forces generated have nowhere to go but inward.

The "Jungle" (#28) mural which follows is dominated by Mr. Foley's African face mask. His declaration, "Help, I'm a rock," focuses the discussion. The group-self has petrified and the group tries to reestablish an identity in a mask. That is, it seeks a false identity, an expression, through Mr. Foley. As he indicates, however, his own condition is such that he has no structure to lend. In the mural, man-eating plants and alligators are present. A cartoon quality detaches the group from its terror as surely as depersonalization keeps a man from the bodily source of his disturbance. The attempt to find a false identity in a mask and the feeling of being turned to stone are typical of the schizophrenic's dilemma. It is significant that the group accepts this theme as its own expression.

By May 11, the group expresses further regression. "Fairyland" (#39) cartoons good fairies and bad witches. The group projects good- and bad-mother images as it seeks protection and substance. The attempt to live in the part object, the image, is carried further in "Transylvania," (#40). The omnipotent, maternal image is made to kill and eat the self, and then to bring it back to life. Miss Allen suggests "Transylvania" saying, "Let's do a little for the outside, and a lot for the inside." The scene portrays the birth of a monster Frankenstein (rebirth of the self) with the bloodsucking "iron maiden" as midwife (maternal image). A genie rising from a bottle repeats the theme of rebirth.

The regression of object relations proceeds straight into "Dreams" (#41) of May 25. A suckling baby is born, and the good-mother proffers the bottle and the breast. The group-self, as baby, goes on to recreate the rebirth fantasy in the "L.S.D." (#42) mural. Disjointed maternal images are the focus of vivid visual excitement. The faces of the self and object are confused mirror images. The group manifests excitement as it participates, in the strong, colorful imagery (black, red and green cones, pinwheels, exploding lights, eyes, etc). The intensity of the visual imagery and the increasing use of faces as the content in the murals points to the resolution of this sequence. The group is seeking to absorb itself into the exciting memory of mother's face. However, as Miss Al-

len's discharge becomes imminent and as Miss Salvatore's wedding and departure from the ward approaches,
there is a prolongation of this stage. It is as if the resolution cannot work if the figures for the projection of maternal imagery are not available.

In the following mural, appropriately called "Funny
Faces" (#43), suggested by the most psychotic patient in
the group, there is a blatant concern with faces and
breast imagery, and there are huge mouths present. The
resolution concludes on June 14 in "Beatles Album"
(#44). The group loses itself in the Beatles imagery just
as it currently loses itself in smoking marijuana on the
ward. The fluidity of images is portrayed when the patients play a trick on the staff by switching seats at the
mural session in order to mix themselves up and to con-
fuse the staff which regularly notes the seating arrangement. The whole period is characterized by a feeling
shared by both the staff and patients that no one is taking care of them. There is a deep sense of longing for
such care.

The aggression which is mobilized by such feelings of
rejection has no external target. Miss Allen and Miss Salvatore must be idealized as "good-mother figures" and
the aggression is bound to images of the "bad mother."
There is increasing fragmentation of the maternal imagery and of the self-imagery until the group dwells almost continuously on images of primary wish-fulfillment.
This takes on an almost hallucinatory quality of the maternal face. The fact that so many people can participate
in this common regression means that each one is mobi-
lizing in himself the regressed images of his own infantile
past. The regression, beyond the psychosis which char-
acterizes many of the group, beyond the drug states
which are being utilized, and beyond the fragmenting
effect of the targetless aggression, draws its imagery from

the world outside of 12-N as well. President Johnson himself is in the throes of seeing his power depleted and "Sgt. Pepper" has taken over the land. Ward 12-N, then, is a "Yellow Submarine" and the group is its crew, searching through the oceans of the unconscious for the promised land of gratification.

In the eighth sequence there is only Ward 12-N. This final sequence begins with a mural entitled "The many faces of Miss Allen" (#45). The group transiently returns in this way to reality, the reality of her departure. The mural illustrates a preoccupation with her face. In the mural the group expresses veiled hatred for Miss Allen, who, having encouraged them to act out their excitement, had ultimately abandoned them. Her final act was to bequeath marihuana. Alternate title suggestions for the Miss Allen mural were "Flower Power" and "False Loves."

Sequence eight proceeds with "Anxiety," representing further aggressive image splitting. It depicts faces of group members (self) and others (presumably maternal images). In this period, with the staff vacations coming up and discharge of many patients imminent, it is no longer possible for the group to trust in the image of any of the others. Insofar as the satisfaction which they have sought in the image of the good mother is no longer possible, they turn their "transference" needs to the institution itself. The "Island" (#47) mural of the unconscious stage portrays the patients in their attempt to find some shelter on the island. They are preoccupied with the means for arriving at such shelter, trying to go by plane, train, boat, messages in bottles, even "pulling the plug," to bridge the gap to the island. As the detailed account discloses, the island portrays the institution at the same time that it represents a very infantile state of being. The following three murals of recombination and resolution attempt to work out this theme. The group is in a situation characterized by the absence of self. Images of the self are dead ("Old Movies," #48, "Brain Damage," #49, and "Mythology in General," #50). In the final mural, "Leaving," (#51), Miss Callahan and a male assistant are going on vacation. Even "Superman" is incapable of saving the group from the silent image of its obliteration.

Object Relations

It will be most illuminating to examine all the data from the standpoint of object relations. Sequences one and two deal with the acquisition of object relationships within the group. The first losses of such relationships in sequence three leads to a deepening of the range of still existing relationships. Group members acquire an empathic sense of the inner life of one another. In this sequence the development of intrapsychic constructions corresponding to lost figures still enhance the group's structural development. In sequence four the group deals with loss of its paternal figure, by attempts to replace him with another reality figure. Although the process of scapegoating substitutes a mental mechanism for confrontation with reality, there is still an adaptive orientation to reality.

Sequence five shows object loss dealt with primarily through individual intrapsychic transformations. As the scapegoat leader is symbolically killed, each group member undergoes a process of identification by which the lost leader is incorporated. In sequence six the group allows its remaining structural cohesion to be overwhelmed. The attempt to recoup the cohesion in sequence seven is largely an intrapsychic pursuit of a fantasied rebirth. The group elevates one of its members to the role of maternal protector. She acts as an outward extension of a commonly held group image of the good mother. Her discharge signals the beginning of a new sequence in which even ordinary images are given up in favor of a combined, unified superimage, which is projected onto the institution as protector.

The first four sequences are essentially a period of structural integration of the group, whereas the last four sequences demonstrate that the same structure is disintegrating. In the following section an attempt is made to show that the process of structural disintegration reverses the process of structural integration which had occurred. The same aggressive forces which are bound under the controlling influence of the Chief of Service and the Head Nurse break loose disruptively in their absence. The resolutions of the first four sequences alter the structural relationship among group members, that is, the set of expectations they have about one another. The resolutions of the latter four sequences involve intrapsychic alterations. In the period of disintegration each sequence reveals the undoing of a step in the development of object relations. In sequence five the object is removed from reality and dehumanized to the status of a symbol thing. In sequence six the body loses its symbolic function to connote a presence that fills it. In sequence seven the image of the maternal face loses its potential to express the presence of gratification. In sequence eight the image of undifferentiated unity loses its ability to express the presence of life. One may perceive the first four sequences and their consecutive undoing in the last four sequences as corresponding to stages in the integration of a developing ego.

In the first four sequences a kind of group ego and self are created. In the second four sequences these are destroyed. This is understandable as the sequences are viewed in the following way. In the first and last sequence the group is undifferentiated and diffuse. In the first case it is the group structure which is diffuse, whereas in the last it is the group mind or image of itself which lacks structure. The second and seventh sequences may be compared similarly. In the second sequence the group attains further structure by identifying itself with a specific maternal subgroup while in sequence seven its undoing is the splitting into good and bad parts of the existing maternal image.

In sequence three the group finds internal cohesion and further substance in reality by responding to the internal needs of one another, while in Sequence six this process is reversed as the group loses internal substance by abandoning one another and thus abandoning its image of itself as a group. In sequence four the group internalizes a father figure through a process of identification, while this is specifically undone in sequence five as the internal image of the leader is dehumanized.

In a general way the development of the ward's structure and identity, occurring over four periods, corresponds to the development of identity precursors in a person. In each period of development a creative synthesis occurs.

Freudian theory holds that the infant's frustration leads to the association of the maternal face and breast with satisfaction or tension reduction. At first, an increase in tension is assumed to provoke an hallucination of an image of satisfaction, but if tension reduction is to occur on a regular basis, the perceptual reality of the infant must be made to accord with the image of satisfaction. That is, the mother must appear. It becomes important to recognize the maternal presence. Thus, the diverse images of mother's face must be integrated into a single representation. Such a synthesis of images into a more unitary integration is one example of the kind of creative integration which must occur in the developing ego. Gradually the image of the source of satisfaction becomes more integrated with reality. In order for this to occur a series of mental integrations is necessary. Such integrations deal largely with an increasing recognition of the real nature of the self and of objects.

The integrations which occur in each of the four periods of the ward's development can be related to the integrations which occur in a person's development. In the succeeding material it will be assumed that the discussion is equally relevant to the group's integration and the individual's. No further attempt will be made to differentiate between the two.

Conceivably the organism's first creative synthesis is the gestalt of the maternal face. Frustration forces the movement away from the unity of the primary narcissism to this recognition. In sequence eight the unity that precedes the mother's face is depicted in the sense of its life-giving property. The next creative task is to integrate the diverse images of that face with a recognizable maternal presence. The apperception of this presence implies some state of minimal consciousness of being, in her image. In sequence seven the image of the maternal face is the main focus. The next creative task is to transfer the sense of being to the image and appearance of the whole body. Sequence six deals with the body's symbolic function of connoting the presence that fills it. Finally, a representation of a symbolic equivalent to the body is synthesized. Sequence five deals with its dehumanization.

In a sense the problem of identity development is the question of, from where does the feeling of life emanate? In seeking satisfaction the organism must turn back to reality and the object thus becomes associated with satisfaction. Each time the real object disappears, an attempt is made to hold on to its image. When the various images of the object are combined, a great deal of mental energy is saved. From an economic point of view it may be stated that rather than cathecting each image separately, the fused image may be cathected with just a portion of the energy previously involved, thus hypercathecting the fused image with surplus energy. This corresponds to Kris' (1952) idea that creative activity results in conservation of mental energy. Thus, the synthesis of images of the maternal face into a permanent representational focus creates a major structural change in the infant's world as well as providing a quantity of energy which can be utilized for attention and consciousness. At this level consciousness arises in the sense of being which occurs when the mother's face fills the world and, conversely, the alteration when she is gone. There must be a feeling of "goodness" when she is present and a feeling of "badness" when she is absent. These are the original feelings of life and they are bound to the image of mother. "Goodness" is being enveloped in her presence and "badness" is the feeling of her image inside without satisfaction and the attendant aggression. Conceivably, the image of the maternal face is hyperenergized, and the presence of the face in reality is sufficient to release some libidinal energy to the organ of conscious perception, where perception of the image occurs. In the case of frustration with that image, or a loss of it, aggressive energy would provide the attention cathexis to conscious perception.

In the next synthesis, energy is saved by binding the images of mother, good and bad, into a unitary structure (sequences two and seven). The next creative integration (sequences three and six) involves a displacement of cathexis of the maternal image to the body of the self. This conserves energy by binding the myriad body feelings and erogenous zones into a single image of the body. The energy which is made available is used to promote consciousness of the body and of the self in relation to the body. It is the sense that the life of the self at this level is acquired from outside.

In the following creative integration (sequences four and five) there is an establishment of a representational world of symbolic equivalents to the body, self and objects. This promotes a further saving of energy and allows a sense of abstract consciousness to come into being. Furthermore, a way of dealing with object loss through symbolic manipulations is acquired.

Creativity and Identification

The self wrests life from the object by drawing the images into its own purview. Such development is analogous to the creative process. When an artist grapples with a problem, he surveys the material, the imagery and the medium of that imagery. He makes it his own by taking it into himself, where he reorganizes, simplifies, makes connections, in an attempt to form a newer, more beautiful integration of it. It is precisely this activity of self, in which the experience of self-discovery lies. The artist, faced with a problem in reality, with his object, with the need for satisfaction, takes the images of the object inside himself, tries to encompass them, to produce a new relationship between them, and between them and himself.

Thus, each creative experience is a recapitulation of development. The stages by which the murals were produced can now be viewed as particular cases within the framework of the creative process.

Each person must be constantly recreating himself out of the substance and experience of his world. Although such an integration may be a mere reintegration of the same components, in identity formation, or illness, or artistic enterprise, a radical new self is formed. Just as an infant expects the important adults in its life to mediate its search for satisfaction, the group relates to its problems in reality with the general expectation that a leader should mediate the solutions. Thus an object is felt to be in the position of channeling the group's efforts at satisfaction. When this does not occur the object is felt to have abandoned the members and it must either be regained, replaced or related to in a different fashion through a change in the self-structure. All of these possibilities come into play in the mechanism of identification. This mechanism mediates the synthesis which occurs at each of the four basic stages of self-development. At this point it is useful to reexamine the six stages which were discussed in the mural sequence. Their coincidence with the stages in the creative process have already been noted but the notion that they comprise the basic elements in the mechanism of identification has not been thoroughly examined. In a general way it has been determined that the group develops structural integrations through a process of acquiring substance from its objects. To ask how the transfer of image material from object to self is effected is another way of asking what the mechanism of identification is.

In Stage One the self (individual or group), frustrated, as if by the object, exerts its full force of consciousness to seek satisfaction. Self-consciousness, object consciousness and reality consciousness are all heightened and clearly demarcated.

In Stage Two a partial regression in the service of the ego ensues such that self and object are portrayed in symbolic terms, thus reduced by a dimension to the status of abstract representations.

In Stage Three anxiety causes a defensive flight from these mental images which are infused with an unpleasant valence. They are repressed.

In Stage Four, after repression, the images of self and object in accord with the laws of the primary process, and in accord with earlier more primitive modes of self-object intrapsychic existence, freely mingle and fuse. The transfer of energy which is the essence of identification occurs at this stage. The aggressive drive, which is experienced in all its derivatives as emanating from the self, is bound to images from the object world. This imbues the images from the object world with a sense of real being. These images develop structural significance as they are bound with aggressive energy.

In Stage Five the transmuted images of self and object are restructured to fit in again with more developed self-structure, adding as they are reabsorbed, a new element to the self.

In Stage Six the altered self reapproaches reality and the real object once again. In the process, the self-structure has absorbed elements of the object. The self is now ready to resume its function of channeling drive energies toward discharge possibilities in reality. An identification has been created. The group becomes the object, representative of all objects, out of which the material for solutions and self-awareness must develop.

In this year of August 1, 1966 to August 1, 1967, the patients on Ward 12-N of the Theodore Herzl Hospital are faced with a communal reality fraught with communal dangers, responsive to communal solutions. They achieve certain integrations in their own structure which deserve to be considered true creative solutions, full of beauty and economy of means. The list of problems and their resolutions bespeaks the beauty of their strivings. The mural medium itself, that cardboard screen, blank as a mind without thought, is the substance upon which the images are projected.

Individual Patients

Three patients are chosen to have their contributions to the group mural discussed in depth. These three, Miss Serena, Miss Allen and Mr. Ronan, are chosen for various reasons. First, in their stays on the ward they overlap the entire year's murals. Miss Serena is active in the mural group from August, 1966, through January. Miss

Allen is a patient from February, 1967, through the beginning of June. Mr. Ronan is a patient from April, 1967, through August. The three also represent different diagnostic categories. Miss Serena is a "borderline" patient. Although relatively intact, she has severe problems in separation-individuation. Miss Allen has a character disorder, but an intact ego. Mr. Ronan is a schizophrenic whose contributions to the mural represent a third level of ego functioning. Each patient has a significant role to play in the mural sessions. All are patients of Dr. Lukens.

Miss Serena is constantly striving to form a separate self-structure. She is at that stage of development where ambivalent anger is used to push the object away in order to allow the self to break free of symbiosis. This is clearly portrayed as she draws large divisions in the murals, often setting up a large portion as her own personal domain. She resents intrusion into this domain except by her own express invitation. She reflects the group's dynamics. She always reacts to the group's dynamic struggles either by joining in, if the group itself is attempting aggressively to individuate, or by sealing herself off if the fusion themes are dominant. The time of her stay on the ward is fortuitous. The task of the group at this time is to come into a kind of individual being, a struggle which Miss Serena can utilize to augment her own search for a separate identity. As a child, her self-development was arrested, but once conditions were amenable to her development she was able to differentiate. This is a typical struggle of the borderline patient.

Miss Allen responds to the mural in an abstract and rather personal way. She differs from Miss Serena in her ability to use the form of the mural to express dynamics of her own, differing radically at times from what the group itself is working through. She still uses the group's struggles to express her own when it is convenient for her to do so. Miss Allen responds to the entire form of the mural. She can let it stand for different aspects of herself. In the "Fence" (#30) mural, for instance, the fence may be likened to her outer boundary; what occurs inside is akin to her own unconscious realm, full of her infantile wishes. What is portrayed outside the fence symbolizes action for her. Miss Allen's contributions to the mural frequently include the floor as well as other structural elements. For instance, she delineates all the semicircular cages in the "Zoo" (#33) mural, the cobblestone road of the "French Revolution" (#31), the tile floor of the "Operating Room" (#32) and the grass of the "Zoo" (#33). This differs from Miss Serena's use of boundary lines by virtue of the higher degree of differentiation in form. Miss Allen can let the whole mural stand for herself, whereas Miss Serena has to segregate off from the whole her part area, her domain. Miss Allen has a rather fixed self-structure, making it possible for her to express feelings in those situations where a more psychotic patient would typically react with structural changes in the personality. She no longer has to concentrate on the preservation of self-structure. The patients become angry with her because she encourages acting out, which her own structural development allows.

Mr. Ronan, unlike Miss Serena, wants to be absorbed and to have his self disappear. He indulges in a regressive splitting up of the self in order to search for the all-protecting, primitive, internal mother. This destructive fragmentation relates to the schizophrenic process. He repeatedly uses the mural to express his helpless, self-destructive, passive themes. The structural disruptions that he proposes—the eyes coming out of mouths or two-faced beings—may have little relation to the organic structure of the mural. When he does relate to the mural

it is to the content rather than to the form. His self-structure is not sufficiently developed to the point where he
can relate to the entire form of the mural.

It is interesting to compare the three patients in their
reaction to anger when that is the dominant element in a
mural. Miss Serena withdraws, or turns the anger onto
the object in order to separate herself from it. On certain
occasions, the threat that she would merge with the object resulted in serious suicidal feelings. When anger is
present in Mr. Ronan's murals he turns it back upon the
self, causing further disintegration in his own structure. A
kind of suicidal impulse is evident here, but it is of a
different form than that which has been described for
Miss Serena. His death denotes the absence of self. Her
death denotes the destruction of the object. Miss Allen
relates to angry themes by using the anger as an impulse
to action. She expresses the anger by activity rather than
by either structural integration or structural disintegration.

Method of Cultural Analysis

A method of cultural analysis is developed here which
bases its conclusions on the following movements and
responses to aggressive forces. A psychiatric ward is used
as a prototype of a relatively self-contained culture. The
Director of the unit and the Head Nurse are seen as the
figures in reality who set external limits on the direction
and flow of aggressive interchange. As events develop in
this culture, they follow shared patterns of individual
processes of ego maturation. Just as limitations in the
flow of aggression can induce intrapsychic structure formation, the same movement in a culture produces
changes in the structure of that culture. The artistic productions both reflect and express the evolution of the
structural development. As each individual participates in

the events of the culture which surrounds him, he makes use of common imagery to relate himself to the other individuals.

Through cultural pursuits, each person tries to recreate himself in terms of common and available symbols. The culture also provides a current available means of handling aggression and, to an extent, each person participates in this. In effect, the structure which is evolved at any particular time in a culture for handling aggression is incorporated by the individual, thereby coming into contact with the emerging wishes and feelings. The conflict between the internalized suppressing forces and the person's own wishes is repeated in each individual, who contributes, each in his own way, to the ongoing conflict in his culture between aggressive forces and the available means of satisfaction. As each person has his place in the formation of resolutions according to his own ability to produce resolutions, each person becomes a symbol in his culture of a particular form of resolution. As culture is incorporated, then, into the individual's mind, each other person is taken into his symbolic context. A kind of inner drama is composed, populated by the people who surround him.

Just as aggression plays an important distancing role in the territorial imperatives of the animal kingdom, so do similar imperatives exist in human behavior. In a sense, the resolutions of aggression provide a means for ordering psychic distance among people. The variety of solutions and the formal relationships which are worked out are well documented here. Intrapsychically as well, the players must conform in their place on the stage to the current set of rules which govern their movements. The choreography of the inner stage is delimited by the dance master of the external stage. Dr. Isaacson's repertoire is limited by his masters as they confront his sense of dance. The ward is his creation, but it is recreated anew by each participant, each of whom hopes to find himself in the structure of the ward.

It should be possible to examine other cultures by following the evolution of their art forms and the movement of their inherent aggressive themes. Perhaps a coherent story of growth can emerge by following such problems and their resolutions for any group.

It would be intriguing to compare the resolutions worked out in each sequence with different political systems. A political structure must deal in large measure with the means of channeling aggression in its domain. On the ward, the designations "liberal" and "conservative" are more than an analogy: they refer to a kind of limited-scale political system. As this system is internalized, it provides means for the individual to channel his aggressive drives.

Implications for Individual Ego Development

Because of the restrictions and frustrations imposed on him, the individual undergoes a process of character construction. In the analysis of the ward's development, each stage has been seen as comparable to a stage of identity synthesis. The aggressive feelings which are mobilized are bound first in an image of the mother's face and body, then in a "body ego," then in a sense of self and finally in an abstract representational self. The aggressive energy which is bound in this way becomes neutralized and in each rather massive integration which occurs a large savings of energy is the result. This neutralized aggressive energy is available to be employed in a more intense consciousness of being. The ego now has available a quantity of neutralized aggressive energy for saying "no" to the drives and for general defensive purposes.

The process of creating the self at the various levels is

ongoing. Just as sleep entails a suspension of the various ego structures, waking recreates them once again. The patients and personnel populating ward 12-N all entered into the process of building a structure for the group. This is made possible because each person can recreate his own identity in terms of the prevailing social order. The process of recreating the self and thus neutralizing aggression is seen as a way of maintaining the ego structure, or at least reaffirming it. Further, it makes available a continuing source of energy for the ego's use. This is a concept analogous to the physiologist's belief that elements in the body are constantly in a dynamic state of replacement. Even bones are constantly reabsorbed and recreated. The elements in the ego structure are seen as constantly disintegrating and reintegrating. In fact, one can postulate the need to maintain and to reshape the ego's structure as a motivating force in coming together and relating individually to one another in a culture.

Conclusion

Essentially, this book develops a method of cultural analysis in which the structure of a culture is seen as being determined by the forms of infantile structure obtaining in the members of that culture. This is a method of analysis which does not specifically try to fathom the transformations of energy, that is, the motivational aspects of development, but rather attempts to describe the formal relationships.

Four meaningful syntheses of identity have been described in their relationship to group formation. It has been pointed out that these are the same syntheses which occur in individual development. It is the thesis of this book that the undoing of the structural integrations represents a process of group schizophrenia. In the last six months of the year, each sequence pertains to the specific

undoing of the level of integration which is most
differentiated and most recent in the development of the
ward. Thus the murals, beginning with sequence five,
show an increasing concreteness. They become pervaded
by an unreal, cartoon quality, not unlike that stage in the
schizophrenic process where depersonalization begins
and a detachment from feeling becomes all-encompass-
ing. In sequence six the group is represented in a "body"
which undergoes disintegration as individual members
complain that they no longer feel physically whole or
intact. There is clear imagery present that represents
this disintegration. This corresponds to the stage in the
process of schizophrenic disintegration where somatic
delusions are present and where the person feels that his
self is no longer a central focus in his existence. In sequence seven the group's maternal image is specifically
undone as it is split once more into "good" and "bad"
components. There is a sense of loss of protection and
a liberation of distressful and disturbing impulses. Drugs
are part of the culture at this point and they sometimes
initiate, but usually follow, the attempt to exist at a less
differentiated level of consciousness where there is hardly
a body, no longer a self and only the wish for a per-
vasive maternal presence. Conceivably, this corresponds
to the time in a schizophrenic disintegration when attempts are made to substitute other objects for the missing self, when delusions of control and persecution and
regressive hallucinations become vivid. The final stage
of disintegration of the group is that in which the maternal image is no longer a focus for existence; rather
there is only a pre-existing, undifferentiated, sense of life.
This corresponds to the final stage in the schizophrenic
process of disintegration where an attempt is made to live
entirely through a kind of fused, impersonal image of
life. In this phase, the chronic schizophrenic may be as
related to an institution as he could be to a particular

person. The point is that neither the institution nor the person provides the schizophrenic with anything more than the sense of being alive. Appropriately, the last mural of the year ends on such a note. Thus this is a case history of an institution: Ward 12-N, Theodore Herzl Hospital, developed an acute schizophrenic reaction.

In one way, this kind of reaction facilitated the therapeutic process in that the elements of schizophrenic pathology in a predominantly schizophrenic group were clearly defined. There was no attempt made to cover them over with rigid rules or veneers of functioning. Dr. Isaacson's philosophy of long institutional stays enabled patients to actually work through in their treatment the various levels of psychopathology. The therapists developed a fair degree of consciousness of the levels of pathology here described and became part and parcel of the therapeutic approach. From one point of view, the initial period of growth and development of the ward group was most helpful to those patients, like Miss Serena, who were themselves in need of a whole process of ego development, one which had never been completely undergone. In late winter and early spring, when aggressive themes were rampant, patients with depressions, even psychotic depressions, managed to do quite well. Here they had the opportunity to turn their aggression outward onto the group structure and to participate in the group's cathartic process. In the final stages, when the group attained its schizophrenic structure, schizophrenic patients actually made a good deal of individual progress.

A Therapeutic Approach

In a therapeutic approach to the group, mural production could be used as an indicator of the level of "ego" maturity of the group. The therapist would have to get his bearings by considering various parameters of the group's function. Experience with the present group suggests that first consideration be given to defining the reason for the group's existence. Second, one must question who is the leader nominally, as well as in reality. Further definition would explore the leader's relation to the group's purpose and the nature of the group's relationship to its leader. These basic questions lead to the nature of the group's real problems. This brings into focus sources of hostility, both from within and outside the group. The method of dealing with such hostility can be recognized by discovering the nature of the group's structural development. If the group has a clear working relationship to its problems in reality, the leader is probably directly concerned with that activity. If the group is more related to its own imagery and its own past existence, its leader is probably in less direct contact with its activity.

From an ego psychology point of view, the group's structural development can be assessed according to its level of maturity. The most primitive integration would be a symbiotic group, using its aggression to keep each member separate, equal, and generally polarized into one of two large "camps." The next level of maturity would encompass a separation-individuation phase where each group member finds definition in the kind of role which he performs. Aggression is used at this level to jealously guard the integrity of the subgroups which have been formed. The third level of group ego maturity would consist of an identification phase in which group members incorporate the image of their leader, and of one another, leading to an empathic sense of sharing the same fate. Aggression at this level is used to enhance the identification process. It is transformed or neutralized in the process of structure formation in the mechanism of identification with the aggressor. It is the communal sense of weakness vis-à-vis the leader which fills his image with a sense of power in this mechanism. The final stage of group ego maturation noted with the present group concerns the development of a sense of representational or abstract existence. The group functions according to principles which it has developed and adopted from its leader, who can be represented by a surrogate figure, or by an abstract principle. The group's aggression at this stage can be united and focussed through its leader figure toward a sense of mastery of the problems of the real world; or the aggression can be focussed back upon the group through a mechanism of common guilt vis-à-vis the leader.

The disintegrating possiblities in the group's structure have been documented and explored; they can be recognized by noting the inner-directed, structural dislocations unleased by aggressive strivings. There is an attempt to live through the images which have been developed in the various phases of the group's development. The nature of the imagery depends on the level of disintegration to which the group has regressed. In such phases the group is no longer related to the function of producing changes in its reality in accord with its needs. In preparing to use the group mural, the therapist would attempt to discover the phase of the group's ego maturity.

The therapist would want to help the group achieve the integrations in its structure for which it is striving. In order to do this, he should tailor his interpretations to the stage of the sequence which the group is currently undergoing. It becomes important to recognize the stage. Each stage has certain formal and certain content-oriented characteristics. In the reality stage, the content deals with the actual presence of the group and with its actual location in space and time. Formally, there is a lack of symbolism and a dearth of artistic expression in the mural. In the stage following, where the problem of the group is stated, symbolism is present but it clearly relates to the group's realistic situation. Animal content is particularly suited to this stage. Animals provide an easy and expressive disguise and the opportunities to express more aggressive feelings are enhanced. In the stage of defense, the content is often expressed in images of flight or movement, or in images of actual places removed from the scene of reality. Anxiety itself may be the theme of this stage. Abstract motifs may also express the flight from reality. The unconscious stage is most easily recognized by the symbolic water or double layering content of the mural. Other direct expressions of this stage are seen in the themes of "emotion" or "dreams." The formal characteristics of this stage include the opposition of large energy forces and the relative invisibility of the real group. The stages of reintegration and resolution are characterized formally by the predominance of free energy, leading to ebullience or relaxation, smoothness and a relative lack of conflicting elements. The group appears in agreement. The content often reveals the group re-emerging toward its actual locale, both spatially and psychologically.

Assuming that the stages can be recognized by the therapist, his remarks should be directed by this understanding. In the reality stage he should help the group define its real problem, accenting its relation to its leader and the nature of its aggressive dilemma. In the stage of symbolism the problem should be redefined using the prevailing content and interpreting the symbols. In the defensive stage the nature of the flight and the kind of defense in use should be pointed out. The whole question of resistance and the position of the therapist as surrogate leader may be pointed out, depending on the purpose of the group, i.e., whether therapy or goal-oriented function is its goal. In the stage of unconscious confrontation the therapist should try to define the way toward solution of the aggressive conflicts. During the reintegrative stage, a rational approach would attempt to apply the resolution of aggressive conflicts to the group's reality situation. Finally, in the stage of resolution the therapist should recall the group's original problem, summarize the movement away from the problem and praise the members for the aspect of resolution. He should help the group relate the resolution of aggression to its present feeling of unity.

With the approach which has been outlined, one hopes to raise the group's level of consciousness of itself and of its own purpose, by giving it the verbal means to express its own life and form as a group. More general interpretation may link sequences in the life history of the group, in order to increase its appreciation of its own continuing maturity or regression as an entity. Ideally the therapeutic aim would enhance the development of a group which is governed by abstract principles that serve its raison d'être. Such a group would become increasingly conscious in each sequence of its existence.

Metapsychological Conclusions

Taking an overview of the changes which occurred in the group leads to some metapsychological conclusions which may have equal validity for the development of intrapsychic structure and for the "ego structure" of a group or institution. When the group undergoes a frustration in reality such that its ability to achieve its goals or to obtain such gratification which it has determined is necessary for its existence, there is an aggressive response. Those elements in reality which are experienced as frustrating are cathected, and their image, having been taken into the "ego of the group," threatens the stability of the self and object structures which are essential within the group or within an individual. Defenses are mobilized and the offending images of reality, as well as the portion of the structure which is threatened, are either repressed or defended against in some other manner, thereby meeting with the unconscious sources of drive energy. In a primary process way, the energy distributions relating to the cathexis of the offending image and of the threatened structure are redistributed. This results in a reorganization or an affirmation of the structure involved, such that it can include the image of the offending elements in its rubric. This structural and energetic reorganization allows the entity to react in a way which is more reality-syntonic. The mechanism which has just been described is the mechanism of identification.

Essentially, the mechanism of identification is seen as a way of structuring aggression which fosters adaptation to reality. As long as the resulting structure is stable and works to neutralize aggression in a socially or personally adaptive way, conflicts with reality can be minimized. If there is a change in reality, that is, in the forces which affect the entity's approach toward its aims, then a structural change occurs through the mechanism which has been elaborated. The authors of this work find that this mechanism is equally explanatory for individuals as well as for institutional groups. One may consider this process as compatible with the general biological process of evolution, that is, the aggressive forces within an individual or institution, as they reach the surrounding reality environment, strive toward adaptive changes. If the changes are maladaptive, then the entity cannot survive in the reality climate which prevails. If aggression is usefully employed in forming adaptive structures, the libidinal and need-seeking aims of the entity are facilitated, resulting in a predominance of this kind of available energy over that of aggressive energy. The walls of the self which are built up in this way organize the experience of the individual or of the group such that one may truly say that there is evolution in consciousness.

BIBLIOGRAPHY

Bach, G. R. (1954), *Intensive Group Psychotherapy.* New York: Ronald Press.

Freud, S. (1900), The interpretation of dreams. *Standard Edition,* 4/5. London: Hogarth Press, 1953.

_____ (1913), Totem and taboo. *Standard Edition,* 13:1–161. London: Hogarth Press, 1955.

_____ (1917), Mourning and melancholia. *Standard Edition,* 14: 237–258. London: Hogarth Press, 1957.

_____ (1921), Group psychology and the analysis of the ego. *Standard Edition,* 18:67–143. London: Hogarth Press, 1955.

Hartmann, H. (1950), Comments on the psychoanalytic theory of the ego. In: *Essays on Ego Psychology.* New York: International Universities Press, 1964, pp. 127–129.

Kramer, E. (1958), *Art Therapy in a Children's Community.* Springfield, Ill.: Charles C Thomas.

Kris, E. (1952), *Psychoanalytic Explorations in Art.* New York: International Universities Press.

Kwiatkowska, H. Y. (1962), Family art therapy. *Bull Art. Ther.,* 1 (3):3–15.

Laing, R. D. (1960), *The Divided Self.* Chicago: Quadrangle Books.

Lewin, B. (1969), *The Image and the Past.* New York: International Universities Press.

Naumberg, M. (1966), *Dynamically Oriented Art Therapy.* New York: Grune & Stratton.

Windels, F. (1949), *The Lascaux Cave Paintings.* London: Faber and Faber Ltd.